Create More Butterflies:

A guide to 48 butterflies and their host-plants for South-east Queensland and Northern New South Wales

By Frank Jordan and Helen Schwencke

Photographs by
Helen Schwencke, Glenn Leiper,
John T. Moss, Bob Miller, Lorna & David Johnston

EARTHLING ENTERPRISES
2005

Cataloguing-in-Publication

Jordan, Frank, 1951- .
    Create more butterflies : a guide to 48 butterflies and
    their host plants for south-east Queensland and northern
    New South Wales.

    Includes index.
    ISBN 0 9757138 0 9.
    1. Butterflies - Queensland. 2. Butterflies - New South
    Wales. 3. Butterfly attracting - Queensland. 4. Butterfly
    attracting - New South Wales. I. Schwencke, Helen. II.
    Title.

    595.7890994

Earthling Enterprises Pty. Ltd.,

PO Box 5167, West End, Qld, 4101, I: www.earthling.com.au

reprinted: 2013, 2017,
        2020 (with cover and other image changes and minor updates)

The photos were supplied by and are copyright to:
HS - Helen Schwencke © GL - Glenn Leiper © BM - Bob Miller ©
L&DJ - Lorna & David Johnston © JTM - John T. Moss ©
Scanning and colour correcting of slides and photos by Amelia Pasieczny & Helen
Schwencke

Desktop publishing and production: Helen Schwencke and Amelia Pasieczny

Cover illustrations by Helen Schwencke. The front cover shows the lifecycle of the
Blue Tiger butterfly (*Tirumala hamata*) and host plant Corky Milk-vine (*Secamone
elliptica*). The back cover is of the Joseph's Coat Moth (*Agarista agricola*) on
Slender Grape-vine (*Cayratia clematidea*). The images are based on Helen's extensive series of Butterfly Lives: lifecycle and ecology interpretation signs available
from: earthling.com.au/butterfly-lives/

Special thanks to:
Lois Hughes for use of her paintings and illustrations in the previous print runs.
Sue Wickenden, Smartype, for her technical expertise with the design for this book.
John Moss, Bob Miller (1956 - 2018), Hanny Schwencke and Glenn Leiper for their
support and with proofreading of the manuscript.
The contributing photographers as listed above.

It is with great sadness that we acknowledge the passing of Bob Miller. Bob made a
very significant contribution to this field, and generously shared his knowledge.

Dedicated, with thanks, to Butterfly & Other Invertebrates Club members over the
years for all their hard work, including, in particular, Daphne Bowden and Rob
MacSloy and those acknowledged elsewhere.

Table of Contents

Introduction

There is something magical about having a butterfly waft into your garden. As it flits from flower to flower, it is hard not to be captivated by its grace and beauty.

This has led many people to grow butterfly-attracting plants in their gardens. These are plants that have flowers of the right shape and colour to attract adult butterflies to their nectar.

Attracting adult butterflies can be effective if there is a nearby source of these butterflies. However, for most people in suburbia, there are not enough butterflies to go around, and the variety of those available is very limited.

Obviously more butterflies and more varied butterflies are needed. So where do butterflies come from?

Every butterfly was once a caterpillar and each butterfly species has its own plant or group of plants on which its caterpillars feed. It is these butterfly-creating plants (or host plants) that are the key to successful butterfly gardening; without them there would be no butterflies.

Many of these native host plants are disappearing as their habitats are lost to development or are overcome by weeds. Some lucky butterflies have managed to adapt to exotic ornamentals and weeds that are closely related to their native host plants. Unfortunately, most butterflies are declining as their host plants disappear.

The good news is that the identity of most of these host plants has been discovered. Even better news is that, by growing these plants, you can attract their associated butterflies to your garden, or local bush regeneration site. When the butterflies come they will lay eggs. These will become caterpillars, then chrysalises and finally become a new generation of adult butterflies. And that means more butterflies.

At times, caterpillars will eat many of the leaves of their host plants and sometimes completely strip all of their leaves. Mostly the plants will recover. Importantly, the butterfly caterpillars (and most moth caterpillars) will not gobble up every single plant in your garden. They will restrict themselves to just the few kinds of plants that they are adapted to. Think of them as nature's unpaid pruners.

Caterpillars eat plants and, for most gardeners, this is a situation that they constantly struggle with. In this struggle, many gardeners resort to pesticides of various types. These pesticides don't discriminate between caterpillars, also killing those that would have become butterflies. If you wish to become a butterfly gardener you must become used to seeing a few chewed leaves, even take pleasure in seeing them and forgo the pesticides. Some of the products used by organic gardeners will also harm caterpillars, for example, products based on *Bacillus thuringensis*.

If you do start to grow host plants and forgo the pesticides, you will start to notice a remarkable thing. Your garden will become a refuge for a lot of other wildlife, admittedly most of it on the small side. Little skinks will hide amongst the groundcovers, native bees will visit the new flowers, birds will come and eat the fruit and much, much, more. You may not be able to have a Bilby or Northern Hairy Nosed Wombat in your garden, but you will have a fascinating nature show.

Many people feel an emptiness that is a direct result of the loss of a relationship with nature. In the western world, people may be well fed and healthy and have the latest technological gadgets, but they feel like caged animals pacing up and down as in an old-fashioned zoo. Get some host plants, put them in the ground, nurture them and stand back and watch the web of life weave its magic in your garden. You will, in a small way, have re-established what our ancestors had – a direct relationship with the land, the plants and the animals.

Numerous people have known the benefit of an association with butterflies. Winston Churchill was one of the more famous of these. He had a lifelong interest that started in his childhood. When he was a prisoner of the Boers, he occupied his time by watching butterflies come and go. When he was in India he kept a butterfly collection. Before and during the Second World War he had a butterfly garden and insisted that some garden beds were devoted to the weeds that were host plants for butterflies.

You don't have to be famous to start a butterfly garden but you may need to be patient and persistent. On the whole, butterfly host plants do not fit the profile of the standard plants sold by nurseries, being neither colourful nor well presented. You may have to enquire at specialist nurseries, such as Fairhill Native Plants at Yandina, for some of them. The Australian (and Queensland) Society for Growing Australian Plants have sections on their websites listing many native plant nurseries and this would be one place to start. Another is to become a member of the Butterfly and Other Invertebrates Club and related organisations, since many members will be growing these plants.

New host plants for butterflies and many other invertebrates are still being recorded. For instance, Martin Bennett recently found a caterpillar of the Orchard Swallowtail feeding on *Phebalium distans* and it eventually pupated on this plant. Other people find new locations for already known host plants, for example, Lloyd Bird found the Woolly Pomaderris (*Pomaderris lanigera*) at Ipswich. These new localities can then be checked to see if the associated butterflies actually breed there.

As an experiment, we planted our small inner city block with a large number of host plants. During the last sixteen years over 40 species of butterfly have arrived, unaided, and have bred in our inner city garden. Some only visited a few times while a few have maintained a permanent presence.

Our experimental plantings attracted a quarter of the approximately 160 butterfly species native to the region. We also only grew about a quarter of the approximately 330 host plants recorded for the region. We should point out here that most butterfly gardens would usually be based around fewer plants. A comprehensive list for the region can be purchased from the Butterfly and Other Invertebrates Club.

With this book we have tried to give our readers an awareness of many local butterflies that may be unfamiliar to them. In the first part of the book we have featured 48 of the larger, more spectacular or unusual ones, or some that need special attention. We considered it especially important to show the caterpillars and chrysalises, as these are an integral part of what the animals are. We have usually only illustrated one of the host plants to make it simpler for those starting out. By all means try some of the others if you wish.

The world of butterflies is a fascinating one, and the best way to find out about them is to grow the host plants and experience them for yourselves in your own backyard. However, it is essential that wild places continue to be conserved, so that the majority of species that are unable to find a permanent home in suburbia can continue to exist. We have included a section on some of these places and their butterflies in the latter part of the book.

The latter part of this book also consists of other chapters that, hopefully, will be of interest. These include easier host plants for beginners, butterflies associated with human food crops, some nature observations and a little about day-flying moths. This part of the book mentions some of the many other species of butterflies not covered by the lifecycle information.

On the whole, we promote the growing of native host plants, of local provenance, in preference to any other plants. This is particularly important where people are doing bush regeneration work. However, we also recognize that this isn't necessarily possible (or may not always be desirable) in a small garden situation or where people are setting up a permaculture garden. Therefore, the information provided covers a range of plants, both native and exotic.

To make the information as accessible as possible to the general public, we have used common names and non-scientific language. In the section covering the 48 butterflies each primary native host plant has its scientific name noted below its photo. All names can be located via the index. The common names for butterflies are taken from Michael Braby's "Butterflies of Australia". Where the plant, usually an exotic, is well-known by a common name, only this is used.

We present this book, and its information, to you as enthusiasts and amateurs. We have been working on butterfly gardening for twenty years now, raising butterfly host plants and photographing butterfly lifecycles. In 1992 we produced a small booklet, Butterfly Magic, which is now out of print. The interest generated by this led us to establish the Butterfly and Other Invertebrates Club in 1994. Having the club, and the dedicated band of voluntary workers involved since its' establishment, has made it possible to accumulate a body of knowledge and make it accessible to the general community. The information presented here would also not be possible without drawing on a rich tapestry of local research and observations recorded over the last 150 years. The contents of this book represent some of this accumulated information.

During this time we have done over 180 information stalls, displays and public talks. Answers to many of the questions raised with us by members of the public are included and result in the anecdotal feel of this book. For those who want to go beyond what we have offered in these pages, we have included a list of resources. Prominent amongst these is the excellent work by Michael Braby called "Butterflies of Australia".

The focus during our involvement has been to encourage more butterflies. This has involved bringing eggs inside, raising and photographing the caterpillars, chrysalises, and emerging or newly emerged butterflies, before releasing them. At the time of emergence, they are likely to sit still for a little longer than normal while their wings are hardening. Being living animals, they don't usually bend to the human will. Just when you have the perfect photograph lined up, the creature changes position, tries to warm itself up by shivering its wings, or otherwise makes itself a difficult subject. On occasion we only had limited opportunities to obtain the photographs. The photos presented here are the end result. These are all of living animals, though a small number are asleep from being cooled down for a short time. Since butterflies are cold-blooded, this simply slows them down and causes no damage.

We encourage you to grow your own butterfly garden and increase your local biological diversity. It's lots of fun, costs very little, and can bring hours of pleasure, enjoyment and amusement.

What's in a name

Something strange happens when you look up the word for butterfly in languages other than English. Even in closely related languages, like Dutch and German, the words for butterfly seem quite unrelated, namely Vlinder and Schmetterling respectively. Compare this with the word for cat which is similar in Swedish, Dutch, Greek, Polish, Italian and German (katt, kat, gata, kot, gatto and katze respectively).

A closer look at the meanings of the words within their own languages suggests a possible answer to this mystery. It seems that butterflies are associated with particular stories in each culture. The stories may remain relatively stable for related cultures. However, the word for butterfly gets associated with different parts within each story.

For instance, the making of butter was an important part of daily life in some areas. Apparently sometimes some of this butter would go missing. A diplomatic explanation for this disappearance was necessary. Conveniently, the yellow colour of common butterflies easily suggested their role in this story. So, in English, we have butterfly which focuses on the butter, Schmetterling in German (via the Czech smetana = cream), which focuses on the cream which makes the butter and Babochka in Russian, which focuses on the old woman who made the butter. No doubt this cover story protected the real culprit in the household.

In Catholic Spain the veneration of the Virgin Mary was a more important story. Hence the Spanish word for butterfly is Mariposa – Mary alights. In ancient Greece we have the observation of the transformation of caterpillars into butterflies, and this was likened to the change of the body to a soul at death. The ancient Greek word for butterfly is Psyche, the word for soul.

The mystery of the many different names for butterflies has drawn our attention away from individual words and back to the stories told about butterflies in many cultures. Storytelling and folktales are no longer a significant part of our daily lives. Whereas in the past, stories that people found useful or entertaining would be told and retold. Today the stories that we receive from TV and the movies are the ones that successfully sell the most products.

When we start growing butterfly plants we re-connect with nature and this, in itself, makes us feel better. However, we are also gently reminded that there is a great tradition of folk and fairy tales that people created about their interactions with nature and between themselves. This vast storehouse of knowledge is also disappearing with modern culture, and people miss it without knowing it.

When thinking about butterflies a story comes to mind. It was retold by Idries Shah, the populariser of the humorous Nasrudin stories. In it a person is waiting at night by the edge of a river. In their boredom they occasionally throw small pebbles into the water. Just as dawn breaks they look at the last of the stones and realize that they are holding a small jewel in their hands. Someone had lost a small bag of jewels and the finder was now left with an empty bag and one jewel. In our ignorance, like the stone thrower, we are losing much that is precious in nature. Luckily, with the information we present here, you have an opportunity to help preserve our "flying jewels" and along with this help maintain the biodiversity of the small, often overlooked animals.

Australian Painted Lady

Vanessa kershawi

Australian Painted Lady butterflies like to fly in open, sunny places and land on the ground with their wings open. At times they are seen with Meadow Argus butterflies in similar locations. These butterflies migrate in a north to south direction, so there is a continual turnover of different individuals through your garden. If you have enough host plants, females may stay a bit longer to lay their eggs. Some of the next generation may also stay for a while to lay more eggs, before also moving on.

Caterpillars build shelters amongst the leaves they are eating by loosely weaving them together. In warm weather they grow from egg to mature larvae in a little over a week. They remain as chrysalises for a week or so before they emerge as the adult butterfly.

Chrysalises are often a beautiful copper to gold colour. The word chrysalis is derived from a Greek word meaning gold, so it is not hard to imagine that the closely related European Painted Lady inspired this name.

Of the several host plants for this butterfly, the Paper Daisy is the easiest to grow. It is often available from nurseries. There are many different cultivars available and these come in shades of white, pink, yellow and red. Most forms are annuals, though some other forms are bushy and can last for several years. The local forms are tougher and are often better at self-seeding.

The flowers provide a good nectar source for the adult butterfly as it passes through your garden. If you hang cut flowers upside down they will dry with the flowers open.

Adult   *HS*
× 1.1

Adult   *HS*
× 0.6

Caterpillar   *HS*
× 0.5

Chrysalis   *HS*
× 1.7

Everlasting or Paper Daisy   *GL*
Xerochrysum bracteatum

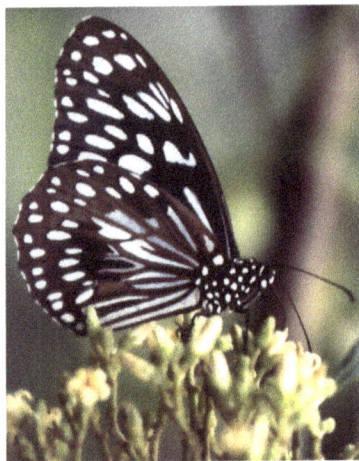

Adult   *HS*
× 0.8

Blue Tiger

Tirumala hamata

Blue Tigers are large and attractive butterflies that are well-known for migrating. In some years vast numbers travel along the east coast. Occasionally some get lost and turn up in New Zealand. If the females find their host plant they lay many eggs before moving on. This may result in the host plant being completely defoliated.

Males have a raised discrete black sex brand on the outside of their lower wings. They sometimes pause at Monkey Rope vines to extract special chemicals from the leaves that make them more poisonous to birds and more attractive to the females. Similar chemicals are found in the exotic Blue Heliotrope (*Heliotropium amplexicaule*). Placing dried pieces of this plant in trees can attract any passing males.

The local host plant, Corky Milk-vine has a milky sap. It is usually found in Hoop Pine scrubs. However the seeds are spread by the wind, and plants can turn up anywhere. The corky, fissured bark of large vines is quite distinctive. The seedpods come in pairs which look similar to the leaves, though swollen, and take a long time to mature.

Corky Milk-vine   *GL*
Secamone elliptica

Seedlings have much thinner leaves than mature plants. Layering of stems near the ground will produce roots at the nodes and these can eventually be separated to produce new plants. In suburban gardens people sometimes grow Yellow Monsoon Bells (*Heterostemma acuminata*). This vine, from North Queensland, has large leaves and is fast growing. However, it is cold sensitive in winter.

Corky Milk-vine bark   *HS*

Chrysalises   *HS*
× 0.9

Caterpillar   *HS*
× 0.7

Blue Triangle

Graphium sarpedon

This butterfly has managed to adapt to suburbia by breeding on the introduced Camphor Laurel as well as native laurels. The leaves of at least one of the native laurels also has a camphor smell. In the past, this tree was often grown as a shade tree in schoolyards and many children have seen this butterfly during their lunch breaks.

The caterpillars and chrysalises are not often visible because they blend in so well with the colour of the leaves. The chrysalises have fine leaf-like lines that closely resemble the veins of the real leaf. As well, just before a butterfly emerges from the chrysalis, its wing patterns are generally conspicuous through the shell, but this butterfly usually emerges at night, so there is no telltale change of colour for birds to see.

Blue Triangles become more numerous a few days after rain. The chrysalises have some way of responding to this and butterflies emerge just in time to mate and lay eggs on the fresh growing tips of their host plants that have been stimulated by the weather change. How they do this is a mystery.

The Three-veined Laurel grows into quite a large tree, as do many of the other laurels that serve as host plants of this butterfly. You will need quite a large amount of room to accommodate one of these trees. The Glossy Laurel (*Cryptocarya laevigata*) is a small tree but, unfortunately, it is one of the few laurels that the butterfly does not usually lay its eggs on. Adult butterflies will sometimes lay their eggs on other unsuitable host plants. Usually these have reddish-coloured young growth, similar to the usual host plants.

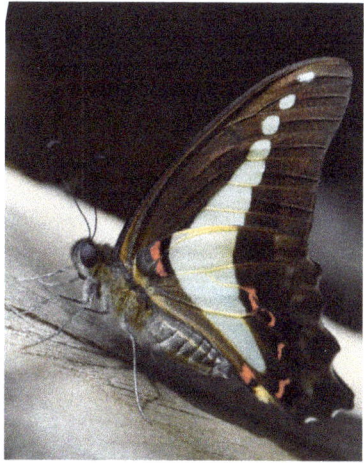

Adult, newly emerged   HS
× 1.1

Adult   JTM
× 0.5

Three-Veined Laurel   GL
Cryptocarya triplinervis

Caterpillar   HS
× 0.7

Chrysalis   HS
× 0.7

Adult   BM
× 1.2

Adult   BM
× 1.3

Bordered Rustic

Cupha prosope

This butterfly is usually found in and around rainforests as this is where its host plant grows. With its wings open it looks similar to the Leafwing though much smaller. It is known to lay its eggs on old spider webs. When the eggs hatch the caterpillars lower themselves down to the leaves. The chrysalis is unusually decorated and may be compared with a Christmas tree ornament.

The host plant is Flintwood. This tree has fruit which are attractive to birds. Some local forms of this plant have sharp spines when small but these are usually outgrown as the tree gets larger. In any case most nursery-grown plants are the spineless forms. The tree can eventually become quite large and also produces suckers.

The caterpillars need fresh young growth. By utilising other species of host plants which produce flushes of growth at different times, it is possible to have a permanent colony in a suburban garden. Dennis Bell uses a combination of five plants in his Brisbane garden. They are Flintwood, *Xylosma terrae-reginae* (a small shrub from SE Qld), *Flacourtia inermis* (a shrub from SE Asia), *Flacourtia* sp. Shipton's Flat (a small tree from Cape York), and *Flacourtia territorialis* (a small straggly shrub from the Northern Territory).

Flintwood   GL
Scolopia braunii

Chrysalis, top view   BM
× 0.9

Chrysalis, side view BM
× 0.9

Caterpillar   BM
× 0.9

Caper Gull

Cepora perimale

Caper Gulls have at least two colour forms, one of which is a mimic of the female Yellow Albatross and the other mimics the Yellow-spotted Jezebel (*Delias nysa*). It can, therefore, be difficult to be sure of the identity of this butterfly when seen on the wing. However, if you see a female laying an egg on a Caper plant then the identification is simple.

Females usually lay their eggs on plants that grow in the shade. Eggs are laid singly rather than in large groups like the Caper White. The green caterpillars are lightly dusted with tiny yellow spots. Chrysalises can be green or brown and are often found on the tops of leaves rather than underneath.

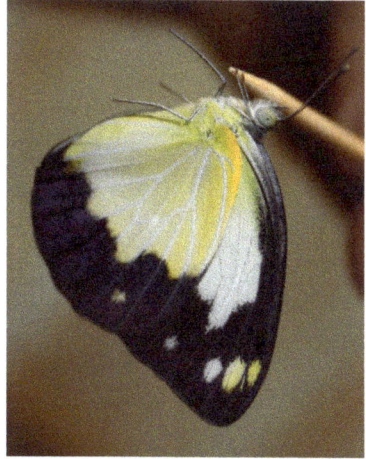

Adult, newly emerged   HS
× 1.6

This butterfly will breed on most species of Caper plants. There are three other butterflies that also breed on Caper plants of various species. Scrambling Caper is illustrated here. Young plants resemble a small-leaved fern though with many small sharp thorns. These are used to clasp to the trunks of the trees it climbs. If it reaches the top and emerges into the light the plant becomes more tree-like with larger leaves.

The plant has a large fruit which is thought to be tasty by some but unpalatable by others. The flower buds of Mediterranean Capers are pickled and used in food. This industry is now being established in Australia. This might seem optimistic considering that the plants can be defoliated by several species of butterfly. However, there are also many predators, such as paper wasps and assassin bugs, that will deal with the caterpillars before they cause too much damage. While the boom-bust cycles of Caper butterflies work to prevent the buildup of these predators, a permanent predator population can be maintained by growing Nasturtiums. These would attract the ubiquitous Cabbage White butterflies to breed and help build predator numbers.

Capparis lucida is a Caper from North Queensland that does not have spines and can be substituted in situations where the spines could pose a problem.

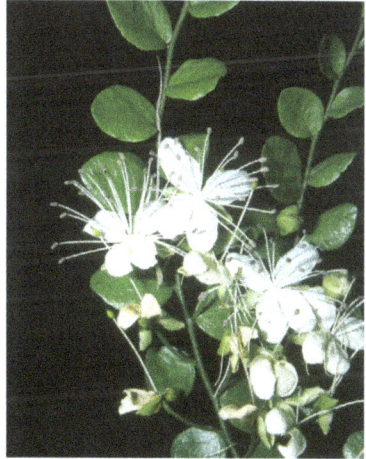

Scrambling Caper   GL
Capparis sarmentosa

Chrysalis   HS
× 1.1

Caterpillar   HS
× 0.9

Caper White

Belenois java

Adult, light colour form   HS
× 1.1

Adult, dark colour form   HS
× 1.2

Caper Whites are another migrating butterfly. They pass through in vast numbers in early summer most years, mostly flying from west to east, after having bred up on *Capparis mitchellii* and *C. lasiantha*, amongst others. Return flights of much smaller numbers are sometimes noticed. They vary in colour from black and white through to black and orange.

Females prefer to lay their eggs on plants growing in the sun. Eggs are laid in clusters. With so many butterflies laying eggs on the same plants at the same time, the caterpillars end up defoliating the plants, though these usually recover.

As with some other butterflies that breed up in large numbers, it can be difficult to tell empty chrysalises from those that will still produce a butterfly. As the shelter provided by the foliage is reduced by the earlier generations of caterpillars, this feature of the chrysalis, by causing confusion, provides a little bit of protection from predators for the latecomers.

Scrub Caper starts life as a spiny shrub and eventually grows into a large tree, similar in appearance to an orange tree. The flowers are scented and short-lived. In those years when the trees have not been defoliated by caterpillars, round green fruit are sometimes produced. Each fruit contains many seeds and these germinate readily, though they are notoriously slow growing.

Capparis lucida, as also mentioned with the Caper Gull, is a spineless alternative for the Scrub Caper.

Scrub Caper   GL
Capparis arborea

Eggs × 9   HS

Chrysalis   HS
one of the colour forms × 1.1

Caterpillar   HS
× 1.0

Chequered Swallowtail

Papilio demoleus

This swift and flighty butterfly is delightful to see on the rare occasions when you are able to get a glimpse. It often keeps its wings moving even while it pauses to sip nectar from a flower.

Caterpillars start off being black and white and resembling bird droppings. As they go through their various stages, called instars, they change to a rusty brown and eventually to green. The chrysalis is either green or pinkish-brown and is directly attached to the plant at the lower end and by a silken girdle about two-thirds the way along its body.

The stronghold of this butterfly is west of the Great Dividing Range where it has several species of host plants. Eventually some butterflies spill out to the coast where they are able to breed on Emu Foot.

Emu Foot is a legume with a deep taproot. It is a goundcover that prefers full sun and spreads out to cover about a square metre. It is easily grown from seed. It is a good idea to soak the seed first to see which ones swell up as these will germinate first. The flowers are small and bluish-purple but occasionally white-flowered plants occur. Western forms of this plant include ones that have much larger leaves and occasionally ones with upright bushy growth habits.

This butterfly has been known to lay its eggs on citrus trees such as limes and sometimes they will be able to complete their development on these plants. Surprisingly in Malaysia this butterfly is called the Lime Butterfly as, there, citrus is its main host plant.

Adult   HS
× 0.8

Emu Foot   GL
Cullen tenax *(formerly Psoralea tenax)*

Caterpillar,   HS   *Chrysalis*   HS   *Adult*   HS
early instar × 1.0   × 0.7   × 0.6

Adult   *HS*
× 1.1

Chocolate Argus

Junonia hedonia

In wet years this large butterfly ranged down as far as Southport, but unfortunately the swamps where its host plant once occurred were filled in and developed long ago. Caterpillars are well adapted to their wetland habitats. Garry Sankowsky has observed that when they had eaten all the leaves on one plant they dropped from the plant and floated to the next plant.

Karamat, its host plant, is usually found growing amongst Melaleucas or along creeks. The plant likes water and can even grow partially submerged. It usually stops growing in winter and dies back to ground level in frosty areas.

Karamat makes a useful addition to a frog pond though it can also be grown in the garden. It is easily grown from seed. Pieces of stem put into a glass of water usually sprout roots and good forms can be propagated in this way.

Its flowers are pollinated by Blue-banded Bees. Small native harvester ants (*Pheidole* sp.) collect the seeds. The Meadow Argus, Varied Eggfly, Blue Argus (*Junonia orithya*) and Dainty Grass-blue (*Zizula hylax*) caterpillars can also utilize this plant.

This plant could be more widely used in the region especially along the drainage channels that were so favoured by water engineers in urban areas.

Karamat   *GL*
Hygrophila angustifolia

Adult   *HS*
× 1.0

Chrysalis   HS
front view × 0.8

Chrysalis   HS
side view × 0.8

Caterpillars   *HS*
× 0.9

Clearwing Swallowtail

Cressida cressida

Male butterflies are usually found leisurely patrolling a patch of host plant. Its relaxed flight is an indication that it is toxic to birds. Females are usually searching through the grass to find their host plants, a small vine called Cressida Pipe-flower. In the process many of the scales rub off her wings, which take on the appearance of the greased or waxed paper used to wrap lunches. The eggs are round and orange and easy to see on the plant.

Cressida Pipeflower is a widespread but un-common small vine. It grows from sea level at Boondall Wetlands up to Mt Nebo west of Brisbane. It is prone to attack by red spidermite in garden situations. The plant produces many black heart-shaped seeds from ribbed seed pods, however, these are difficult to germinate. Propagation from cuttings is easier. Die back occurs during dry weather, but an established plant usually shoots back when it rains.

Adult male   *HS*
× 0.9

Adult female   *HS*
showing transparent upper wings × 0.8

Observant bushwalkers will have noticed that large infestations of the exotic Dutchman's Pipe (*Aristolochia elegans*) will usually be attended by several of these butterflies. Some of the caterpillars can complete their devel-opment on this plant by eating flowers and only the less toxic parts of the leaves. The Dutchman's Pipe should not be grown as it is a serious weed.

If you are seeking an alternative host plant for a garden, this butterfly will also breed readily on the more vigorous native Tagala Vine (*Arist-olochia acuminata*) from North Queensland. En-sure that some of the leaves are close to the ground otherwise the female will not find the plant.

Caterpillar   *HS*
with parasitic Tachnid fly × 0.9

Chrysalis   *HS*
× 1.0

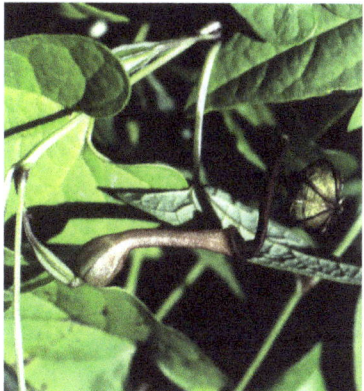

Cressida Pipeflower   *GL*
Aristolochia meridionalis

Rockledge Daisy,　　　　　　　　HS
with butterflies feeding on flowers
Gynura drymophila

Adult　　　　　　　　HS
× 0.7

Monkey Rope　　　　　　　　GL
Parsonsia straminea

Common Crow

Euploea core

This butterfly is the one most remembered from childhood for its bright silver or gold chrysalis found on Oleander plants. Once it was also called the "Ricey" due to its white spots. Its caterpillar is called "Mr. Curley".

Adults usually disappear in winter to join colonies passing their time in sheltered places. Mostly these are small groups but occasionally there are quite large aggregations, reminiscent of those of the Monarch in America.

Sometimes the chrysalis turns black and develops a small hole with a thread hanging down. This happens because, instead of a butterfly, a parasite has developed in the chrysalis.

Monkey Rope is the usual host of the Common Crow in local bushland. This vine also produces large numbers of small yellow-green flowers that are good nectar sources for a large variety of insects including butterflies, bees, wasps, and beetles. Place it where it can be easily viewed.

In a suburban garden this plant can be rampant and may need regular pruning as it becomes large over time. In some bushland areas it is becoming more common. Bushfires are likely to have kept it in check in the past.

A Weeping Fig (*Ficus benjamina*) in a pot would be a suitable non-toxic host in a classroom, or for a balcony. In the early days of Brisbane this tree was grown to shade tethered horses. *Hoya* spp., *Mandevilla* spp. and *Stephanotis* spp. are some other host plants.

Caterpillar　　　　　　　　HS
× 0.5

Chrysalis　　　　　　　　HS
× 1.0

Common Pencilled-blue

Candalides absimilis

Of the approximately sixty-three small bluish and copper butterflies in the region, the Common Pencilled-blue is one of the most ubiquitous.

Female butterflies lay their eggs on the fresh new growing tips. The caterpillars feed on fresh young leaves or flower buds of a wide range of plants. They have an unusual triangular shape that makes them harder to see on the new shoots. The caterpillars can be green or even reddish on those plants with young reddish growth.

As can be seen from the photo, the chrysalis has an interesting shape. In spring and early summer the adult will emerge from the chrysalis in one to three weeks. Those caterpillars that pupate later in the season won't emerge for about nine months to once again lay their eggs on fresh growth.

The Tuckeroo is a common host plant for this butterfly. It is a hardy tree that became fashionable as a street tree and is used by many of the other small blue butterflies that need flower buds or fresh shoots. Its small flowers are pollinated by native stingless bees. The seeds are sometimes used as a food source by the caterpillars of the Bright Cornelian butterfly (*Deudorix diovis*).

Many of the caterpillars of blue butterflies need special ants to look after them. While Common Pencilled-blue caterpillars are sometimes attended by ants, they usually do quite well without them.

Flame Tree, Queensland Nut (*Macadamia integrifolia*) and Black Bean (*Castanospermum australe*), are some other host plants for this butterfly.

Adult   HS
× 1.7

Adult female top   JTM
Adult male bottom × 1.8

Tuckeroo   GL
Cupaniopsis anacardioides

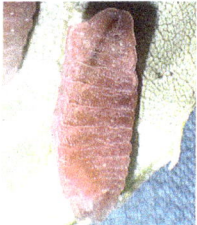

Caterpillar   JTM
often green × 2.1

Chrysalis   JTM
× 2.1

Adult, newly emerged   HS
× 1.0

Finger Lime   GL
Citrus australasica

Caterpillar   HS
× 0.9

Chrysalis   HS
× 1.2

Dainty Swallowtail

Papilio anactus

This butterfly is one that has adapted to exotic citrus species, such as mandarin and orange. These have large flat leaves on which the caterpillar stands out. Its native host plant, Finger Lime, on the other hand, has numerous small leaves on which the caterpillar is well-camouflaged. Nevertheless, this butterfly will happily breed in urban areas. It is not as common as the Orchard and Fuscous Swallowtails which also feeds on citrus.

Finger Lime is a slow growing tree. It responds to fertilizer, particularly well-composted cow manure. It also likes a moist but well drained soil, and is sensitive to dry conditions which will cause it to stop growing and even die back.

The tree is covered in numerous sharp spines. This, together with its slow growth, produces short bushy shrubs which are well liked as nesting sites by small birds.

The fruit is edible but sour and tangy like a lemon. Like the lemon it can be made into a refreshing drink. Unlike a lemon, when you cut the fruit in half, the juice sacs spill out like a bunch of small pearls. The skin colour of the fruit can vary from green to yellow to red. Selected forms are available from nurseries.

The Dainty Swallowtail can be confused with the male Clearwing Swallowtail because both have a similar colour pattern. This is a warning pattern and, in the case of the Dainty Swallowtail, is thought to warn of citrus oils which some predators find distasteful. The Clearwing is warning of the toxins it has collected from its *Aristolochia* spp. hosts.

Adult   HS
× 0.7

Eastern Dusk-flat

Chaetocneme beata

This pretty butterfly has striking red eyes. It is usually not seen during the day because it shelters on the underside of leaves. It is dusk-flying and is sometimes attracted to lights at night. Young caterpillars cut out a piece of leaf and fold it over themselves to create a shelter. As they get older they fold whole leaves over or sew two leaves together with silk. They pupate in their shelters. The chrysalis has a distinctive white patch on its side.

The unusual shelters make the caterpillars much easier to find than the adults. These shelters are often the first indication that they occur in a particular location. The caterpillars are mostly found in rainforest or in shady places along the edges of creeks.

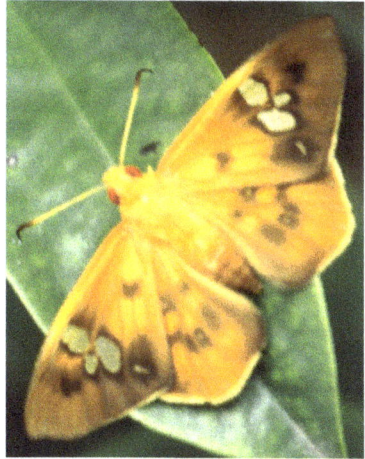

Adult male   HS
× 1.4

This butterfly species has several host plants, the most interesting of which is the Bolwarra. This primitive flowering plant is also called Native Guava or Copper Laurel. Guava refers to its edible fruit and copper to the colour of the foliage in cold weather. It grows well in a garden and produces scented flowers and a fruit which some people say is edible.

A Bolwarra grown in our garden at West End has not produced any ripe fruit, probably because the flowers have not been pollinated. The flowers are unusual because they are pollinated by a special beetle. Some other primitive plants, such as some cycads, are also pollinated by beetles.

Sometimes Blue Triangles lay eggs on this plant. However, the caterpillars eventually die.

Bolwarra   GL
Eupomatia laurina

Caterpillar   HS
× 1.0

Chrysalis in leaf shelter   JTM
× 1.2

Shelter constructed by   HS
young larva × 1.1

Adult, dry season form, freshly emerged   HS × 1.2

Kangaroo Grass   GL
Themeda triandra

Evening Brown

Melanitis leda

Normally active at dusk, this well-known butterfly is often flushed out, during the day, by people walking in the bush. Once disturbed it flies around erratically for a while, then lands and merges with the leaf litter. The adult Evening Browns are attracted to fermenting fruit rather than nectar and may be found frequenting compost heaps. Caterpillars are green and are well-camouflaged in the grasses on which they feed. They have two horns on their head. Eggs are usually laid in shade or semi-shade.

This butterfly has little defence except its camouflage and this is probably why it does not fly during the day. Birds like Willy Wagtails, which are also active at dusk, chase and easily catch these butterflies.

Kangaroo Grass is the most common of the many grasses and sedges that are host plants of this butterfly. This grass has many growth habits, ranging from large to small plants. Try to obtain one of the shorter forms for suburban gardens as the larger ones may become a fire hazard if they dry out. A large clump can easily be divided to produce many smaller plants. Seeds may require special treatment like "smoke water" to germinate successfully.

Try to avoid an exotic grass called Whiskey Grass (*Andropogon virginicus*) which is similar to Kangaroo Grass and has naturalised in many places. Apparently it was used as packing for the whisky bottles for American soldiers during WWII.

Adult, dry season form   HS × 0.6

Chrysalis   HS × 1.1

Caterpillar   HS × 0.8

Four-barred Swordtail

Protographium leosthenes

Rarely seen in urban areas, this attractive butterfly can build up in large numbers where its host plant is common. Its main habitat is rainforest.

Newly hatched caterpillars need very fresh, soft young growth to start feeding, so don't expect any breeding in dry periods as the older leaves are too tough. Caterpillars grow quickly and range from green to dark brown. Chrysalises are well camouflaged in the leaves of its host plant, but seem far too small to produce such a large butterfly.

Chrysalises can last for many years before the butterfly emerges. This is called diapause. Adults are relatively short-lived and chrysalises are somehow able to time their emergence to coincide with the growth flushes of their host plant.

The host plant of this butterfly is Zig Zag Vine, due to the stems occasionally have sharp changes of direction. This plant is usually grown from seed and the plants grow slowly in the first few years. This plant can be pruned to form a bushy shrub, which maximizes the number of soft growing tips, but may reduce the amount of fruit.

The orange fruit is considered to be one of the better native fruits. They are tangy to taste and have a slightly perfumed smell. Each flower can produce a large cluster of fruit.

This butterfly must also share its host plant with the Pale Triangle. Being larger, Pale Triangle caterpillars can use slightly older leaves to start feeding on as newly hatched larva, and so it has an advantage later in the season.

Adult   HS
× 1.0

Adult   HS
× 0.6

Caterpillar   HS
× 1.3

Chrysalis   HS
× 1.0

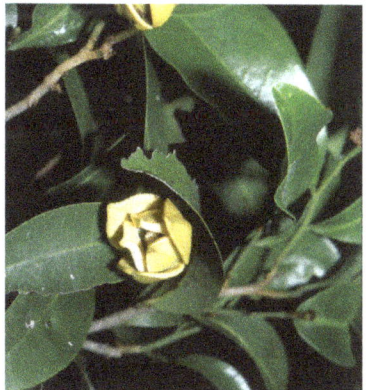

*Zig Zag Vine (**Melodorum leichhardtii**) GL
(formerly **Rauwenhoffia leichhardtii**)*

Adult   HS
× 0.9

Lime Berry   GL
Micromelum minutum

Fuscous Swallowtail

Papilio fuscus

Sometimes mistaken for a male Orchard Swallowtail, this butterfly has distinctive tails but these can be difficult to see when it is flying at any speed.

Eggs are usually laid on fresh growth, and are the usual spherical shape common to all of the swallowtails. This caterpillar, like a number of other swallowtails, also resembles a bird dropping when young. Caterpillars also produce an osmeterium when disturbed (see p. 69).

Chrysalises are shaped and coloured like a leaf with vein-markings, making it difficult for birds to find them. If you raise a batch of caterpillars you will find that most of the chrysalises will emerge within about a month. However, a small proportion will remain as chrysalises for one, two and rarely three years (called diapause). This is an adaptation to Australia's erratic climate. Should there be a few years of drought resulting in no fresh growth for the young caterpillars, a few butterflies will still be around when the rain returns. It can be nervewracking to safeguard these chrysalises for several years until they emerge!

Lime Berry is one of several hosts for this butterfly. It is an attractive shrub that has the added bonus of producing large masses of small white flowers. These are attractive to butterflies of many types, especially the swallowtails. Masses of red berries follow the flowers. In some gardens this plant will perform splendidly, putting on a great show but in others it will be straggly and uninspiring. Good luck with yours.

Chrysalis   HS
camouflaged × 0.4

Chrysalis   HS
camouflaged × 0.4

Caterpillar   HS
× 0.7

Glasswing

Acraea andromacha

Glasswings, like some other butterflies that are toxic to birds, have a relaxed floating flight. The wings are mostly clear or white and black with just a bit of yellow. Occasionally both a dark form and another that resembles the Lesser Wanderer occur.

Eggs are laid in groups of about forty, resulting in many caterpillars on the one plant, particularly if females have laid several batches of eggs. Caterpillars may defoliate a small plant. If this happens in the bush the caterpillars will move off and search for Spade Flower (*Hybanthus stellarioides*) plants on which they can complete their development. Blunt-leaved Passion Vines and Spadeflowers often grow together.

Caterpillars are a plain orange or brown with lightly branched spines. Chrysalises are a work of art with bold black lines on a cream background. They also have a reddish tinge when they have fed on Blunt-leaved Passion Vine.

The Blunt-leaved Passion Vine is one of the native hosts of this butterfly. It has large pinkish flowers that slowly turn red. The fruit falls to the ground where they soften and provide food for Blue-tongue Lizards, which spread seeds around.

The seeds can be difficult to germinate. Alternating wet and dry periods seem to produce the best results. This can be achieved by a weekly sprinkling of the places where there are a lot of fallen fruits. One person recommended the practice of commercial passionfruit farmers, who germinate seed by cutting a fruit in half and placing the halves open side up in the ground.

Blunt-leaved Passion Vine can eventually cover a large area but most gardeners treat it as an annual. This plant also grows easily from cuttings. It is prudent to ensure an ongoing food supply for the batches of caterpillars. Some-times defoliation will even result in the death of your plant.

This butterfly is reasonably common because it has adapted to exotic weeds like the Corky Passion Vine (*Passiflora suberosa*).

Adult HS
× 1.3

Blunt-leaved Passion Vine GL
Passiflora aurantia

Caterpillar BM
× 0.7

Chrysalis HS
× 1.8

Adults, mating   HS
× 1.5

Early Black Wattle   GL
Acacia leiocalyx

Imperial Hairstreak

Jalmenus evagoras

Caterpillars of this remarkable butterfly are tended by a particular type of black ant called the Kropotkin Ant (*Iridomyrmex* sp.). Sometimes there are so many ants looking after a caterpillar that they entirely cover the caterpillar. In return for protection from predators and parasites, the caterpillars provide secretions that the ants find nutritious.

These ants also tend other insects such as leafhoppers. This type of relationship where both parties benefit is called mutualism.

The many types of wattle that are used as host plants are very common. The female will only lay her eggs on wattles that have colonies of the right ants. Wattles about two metres tall are favoured. Where a colony exists, some adults are usually in the vicinity of the host plant where they can easily be viewed. The ants become inactive in winter and the butterflies usually survive this season as eggs laid near the base of the trees.

Early Black Wattle is a common host plant in Brisbane. It is easily grown in full sun or part shade. If grown for the butterflies it will need to be pruned if it gets too tall.

Currently there are no suppliers of the ants so you will need to be lucky and already have a colony of the ants on your property. Some people have succesfully relocated colonies from development sites. During wet weather, colonies will move up into small hollow logs or hollow bamboo stems which can then be relocated. Digging up an ant nest usually results in the death of the colony.

Chrysalis   HS
× 2.1

Caterpillars × 0.5   HS
covered by attending ants

Caterpillar   HS
× 1.7

Indigo Flash

Rapala varuna

The beautiful iridescent indigo colour of this butterfly is not usually seen because it keeps its wings closed when at rest. However, if your host plant is large you will be able to breed many in your garden.

Caterpillars are unusual because of their many small projections. They start by eating the flower buds and progress to soft new leaves as they get bigger. If you raise the caterpillars in a container give them plenty of room and don't let the food run out. If stressed in this way they quickly become cannibalistic.

The eye-spots and tails on the wings can make it difficult for birds to work out which is the animal's real head. By rubbing its wings together the tails also move around enhancing the illusion. Losing a small part of their wings is preferable to being completely eaten by a bird. Proof that this strategy works is demonstrated by the number of small blue butterflies missing these bits of their wings.

Millaa Millaa is the preferred host plant because it produces flowers over a long time. You will also find them breeding on Soap Tree and male Macarangas (*Macaranga tanarius*).

Millaa Millaa is a scrambler which has a growing habit similar to Bougainvillea and can grow equally large. The silvery-gold colour under the leaves is attractive and becomes noticeable on windy days. If you are lucky enough to have fruit on your plant then you are in for a treat. The fruit is tasty even though the seed is large.

Adult   BM
× 2.0

Millaa Millaa   GL
Elaeagnus triflora

Caterpillar   BM
× 1.6

Chrysalis   BM
× 1.6

Adult   HS
× 1.5

Adult Jezebel Nymph   HS
× 1.1

Adult Black Jezebel × 1.1   HS
Delias nigrina

Jezebel Nymph

Mynes geoffroyi

Jezebel Nymphs are usually rainforest butterflies where they breed on several species of stinging trees. At times the population builds up and they move out to breed on Native Mulberry at rainforest edges. This enables the population to really increase so that they sometimes turn up in urban areas. Eggs are laid in batches of about forty and in this way a small tree can be quickly defoliated, eventually exposing any remaining caterpillars to predation by birds.

Adult butterflies are mimics of the Black Jezebel which is distasteful to birds. The chrysalis bears a resemblance to a (tiny) resting fruit bat and even has two shiny spots that look like eyes.

Native Mulberry is a fast growing pioneer species with separate male and female plants. Female trees bear masses of small white berries for about six months of the year. Trees can be heavily pruned to keep them smaller for longer. Though related to the stinging trees, Native Mulberry is safe to touch. One of the forms found in nurseries has stems which, when cut and placed in water, will sprout new roots. This makes it easier to propagate female trees. Otherwise they are usually grown from seed.

This species supports many other types of insects, such as Hedge Grasshoppers, and reptile keepers grow it for this purpose. Birds such as Scaly-breasted Lorikeets also eat the small berries.

Native Mulberry   GL
Pipturus argenteus

Group of young caterpillars
× 0.4   HS

Group of chrysalises
× 0.6   HS

Group of mature caterpillars
× 0.8   HS

Laced Fritillary

Argyreus hyperbius

This highly endangered butterfly was last officially recorded in Queensland in 1992. In the 1800's it occurred from Rockhampton to Newcastle. The female is a mimic of the Lesser Wanderer and derives some protection from its resemblance to this distasteful (and poisonous) butterfly. Laced Fritillaries were usually found in places where its Arrowhead Violet host plant occurred and where there were also populations of the Lesser Wanderer.

In captivity (permit required) the caterpillars will accept both other native and introduced violets. Do not let the food run out as these caterpillars become cannibalistic when stressed in this way.

The Arrowhead Violet is a widespread small herb, though it is becoming rare in coastal areas. Its flowers come in a range of colours from white to pink to purple. Occasional forms also have the traditional violet scent and some have purple undersides to their leaves like Love Flowers. This plant produces proper flowers in late winter and spring, however, during the rest of the year it produces closed, self-pollinating flowers without petals.

The Violets grow very well in pots but can be difficult to grow in the ground. Propagation is usually by seed. Collect it just after the pod opens but before the seeds shoot out. Forms from coastal areas are more erratic in germination than those from the hills. Self-pollinated seed is usually true to type but, if you want to propagate a particular form, try root cuttings. Small butterflies and honeybees pollinate the flowers.

Adult, newly emerged from chrysalis L&DJ × 1.2

Arrowhead Violet   HS
Viola betonicifolia

Caterpillar   L&DJ
pupating   × 0.8

Chrysalis   L&DJ
× 1.1

Some of the variety of violet flower types
HS

Adult   BM
"dry season" form × 1.8

Breynia   GL
Breynia oblongifolia

Chrysalis   BM   *Caterpillar HS*
× 1.4   *× 1.0*

Large Grass-yellow

Eurema hecabe

This bright and cheer-inspiring butterfly makes a welcome addition to any garden. They breed quickly and can build up to a large number of individuals. They also migrate and considerable numbers can appear at times. In our garden they usually arrive in autumn and breed one last generation before winter. These then hide in the shrub-bery during winter emerging on sunny days to sip nectar from Arrowhead Violet and other flowers.

The yellow colour is interesting as an example of recycling. It is partly made up from some of the waste products (pterine) that accumulated in the chrysalis. The rest of this waste is released just after a butterfly emerges from its chrysalis and is usually reddish coloured. One can easily imagine how thousands of butterflies emerging from their chrysalises hanging from trees could lead to stories of raining blood.

The thin white eggs are laid on the soft growth of its host plant. Caterpillars rely on their green colour to avoid predation. Males are able to identify female chrysalises and will sometimes be seen waiting patiently nearby or fighting off other males until the female emerges.

This butterfly has many host plants. Breynia, a shrub growing in the understorey of eucalypt woodland, is a common host. It grows well in a garden though sometimes suckers. Forms with bright red berries as well as black berries are now available from nurseries.

There is some variation in the colour of adults due to temperature variation. Caterpillars reared at lower temperatures tend to produce butterflies with more brown on their wings, as in the illustration.

There are five different species of Grass-yellows in our region and it can be difficult for us to tell them apart when they are on the wing. If they are laying eggs it is easier, as some host plants are specific for each butterfly species. The butterflies themselves have it a bit easier. They use ultraviolet light reflectance patterns to tell each other apart. When humans use special cameras, these different ultraviolet wing patterns are revealed.

Leafwing

Doleschallia bisaltide

Sometimes confused with the Evening Brown, this butterfly goes one better in imitating a leaf by having a fake midrib and stalk. At times it can also be seen basking with its wings open, revealing the bright orange patches on its wings. Like many related nymphalid butterflies, the adults have only four functional legs. This is natural.

The caterpillars are very spectacular and much larger than would be expected after feeding on Love Flower, a small herb. In the bush the caterpillars often travel large distances between plants.

The practice of sheet mulching in revegetation projects does not favour the propagation of this plant. However, it is easily re-introduced once the trees are successfully established. Weeds are also a problem because they can shade out this small plant.

Love Flower grows well in pots, so well that orchid enthusiasts refer to it as Kirkwoods Curse due to its ability to self-propagate in their orchid houses. When the seedpod opens the four seeds can travel several metres. Like the Arrowhead Violet, after the main flowering period is over, it also produces seed without producing flowers with petals.

There is a multitude of forms suited to a wide variety of conditions ranging from stony ridges to deep rainforest. Flower colours range from white to pink to lavender. Many forms have a deep purple colour under their leaves. It can be difficult to believe that all these forms are the one species of plant. They all cross-pollinate happily, usually with the help of Blue-banded Bees.

Adult   HS
× 1.0

Adult   HS
0.7

Caterpillar   HS
× 0.8

Chrysalis   HS
× 0.9

Love Flower   GL
Pseuderanthemum variabile

Adult, one of the many colour forms   HS
newly emerged   *x1.0*

Brush Cassia   GL
Cassia brewsteri *var.* **marksiana**

Lemon Migrant

Catopsilia pomona

These butterflies can complete their lifecycle in a short time. This makes them useful to raise for children who are often impatient for quick results. The caterpillars are green with black and cream stripes along their sides. The green chrysalis shows the support sling typical of this group of butterflies.

Vast numbers can breed in the northern parts of its range and many will head south, some even reaching Sydney. The chrysalises can't survive very cold conditions in winter and each year southern populations are re-established by new arrivals.

When large numbers arrive in a migration they usually end up stripping all the leaves from their host plants. This can make it difficult to grow host plants to a reasonable size without transferring caterpillars to another host plant.

The adults are unusual because they come in several different colour forms from lime green to yellow to white and one even has a bit of red on the wing. There are two main types of patterns, the light coloured "wet season" forms and darker "dry season" forms. The darker forms are more common at lower temperatures.

Native host plants include three varieties of *Cassia brewsteri*, the one illustrated, var. *marksiana* is the most attractive. They can all eventually grow into large trees. They are often available from nurseries and can be grown from seed.

The exotic tree, Golden Rain (*Cassia fistula*), is used by this butterfly and Rowland Illidge noted its use by the butterfly in Brisbane as far back as 1898.

Adult, × 0.6   BM
one of the colour forms

Adult, × 0.7   HS
one of the colour forms

Adult, × 0.7   HS
one of the colour forms

Caterpillar   HS
× 0.6

Chrysalis   HS
× 0.5

Lesser Wanderer

Danaus petilia (formerly D. chrysippus)

Though this is one of the most widespread butterflies in Australia, it has bred in our suburban garden only once in fifteen years. It is basically an inland and northern butterfly which comes to breed in the low lying coastal areas where its usual host, the Mangrove Wax-flower Vine (see Swamp Tiger), grows. Nowadays it also breeds on exotic Milkweeds.

The caterpillars are more colourful than those of the Monarch which also breed on Milkweeds.

A milky sap is produced by these plants. This glues up the mouthparts of chewing insects. To reduce the flow of this sap, often a caterpillar will cut the main vein of a leaf before eating it.

Chrysalises can be either green or pink. Male butterflies can be recognised by small black brands on the lower wings.

Scented Tylophora is a local vine usually found at higher altitudes. It is an uncommon plant and can grow up into the tree canopy where the butterfly is unlikely to find it. We have used it and the related Bearded Tylophora (*Tylophora barbata*) to raise caterpillars in captivity.

The usual native plant used by this butterfly is the Mangrove Wax-flower Vine. It is sensitive to frost. Most gardeners grow one of the introduced Milkweeds for this butterfly, but some local councils have banned either one or more of the common species as they are toxic to horses.

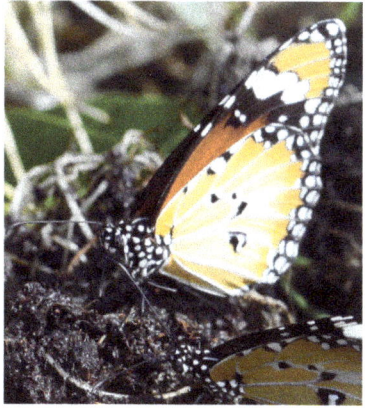

Adult, puddling for water and nutrients   HS × 1.2

Adult   HS × 0.6

Caterpillar on Silkpod flower   HS × 0.8

Chrysalis   HS one colour form × 0.7

Chrysalis   HS one colour form × 0.8

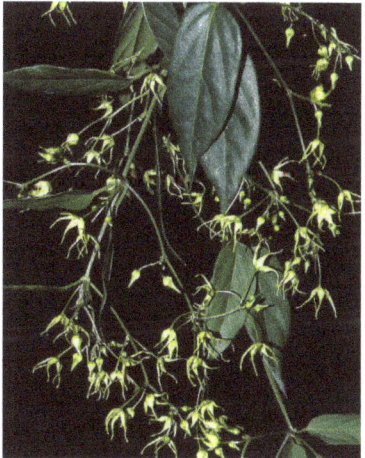

Scented Tylophora   GL
Tylophora paniculata

Adult   HS
× 1.0

Adult   HS
× 0.6

Macleay's Swallowtail

Graphium macleayanus

It is a wonder why most butterflies are not green as it would certainly make them harder for predators to find. The greenish colouration works well for this butterfly as it is the only swallowtail butterfly to occur all the way to Tasmania.

Caterpillars are similar to those of the Blue Triangle and, sometimes, both species feed on the same host plants. Their green chrysalises, complete with a vein pattern, are a good imitation of a leaf.

Macleay's Swallowtails were once much more common in lowland areas when many large creeks still had an edging of rainforest. The butterfly can still be found in those patches of rainforest that have escaped clearing. Creation of wildlife corridors along creeks will greatly benefit this species, especially if an effort is made to include its host plants in any bush regeneration work.

In the 1960s Glenn Leiper observed this butterfly hill-topping (see p. 60) at Newmarket in Brisbane. A bowl of wine attracted some to ground level.

Murrogun is one host plant used in the lowland areas. This can grow into a large tree and is propagated from seed. It is also a host for the Blue Triangle. The black fruit are eaten by some birds. It is likely that this plant will only be used as a host where it is in a sheltered, rainforest type of situation.

G Lyell in 1890 reported that this butterfly would settle near the edge of water and reverse into it, submerging its abdomen and lower wings. Certainly this is an interesting way to cool off.

Murrogun   GL
Cryptocarya microneura

Chrysalis   HS
× 0.9

Caterpillars   HS
× 0.7

Meadow Argus

Junonia villida

With a liking for open spaces, this butterfly frequently settles on the ground with its wings open. It often flies with the similar looking Australian Painted Lady and can be distinguished from it by large eyespots on the inside wings. It has been shown in experiments that the sudden appearance of eyespots, more than any other shape, startles birds.

Mostly observed migrating in a north to south direction, sometimes individuals will linger in the garden for a few weeks or pass through quickly after laying a few eggs. Eggs are usually laid on plants growing in full sun.

The illustrated host plant, Crenate Fanflower, is often available from nurseries because it has attractive small mauve or pink flowers. It also suckers, so can form a short but dense groundcover. Unlike many of the other host plants, this one is dense enough to hide the feeding caterpillars from birds.

At times this butterfly is spoilt for a choice of place to lay its eggs. Even Snapdragons are amongst a range of its host plants.

One of its recorded host plants is Lantana. It is surprising that the Meadow Argus has not been enlisted in the effort to control this plant. Because it migrates in large numbers, it could overwhelm its predators and parasites and cause significant defoliation. There would need to be a program of selective breeding for a preference for Lantana and a mass release at the beginning of a migration.

Adult   HS
× 1.8

Adult   HS
× 1.1

Caterpillar   HS
× 0.9

Chrysalis   HS
× 1.3

Crenate Fanflower   GL
Scaevola albida

Adult   HS
× 0.8

Monarch

Danaus plexippus

This large orange and black butterfly is familiar to many people because it features in much of the butterfly literature originating from America. It is also a popular butterfly in New Zealand.

The main host plants for the Monarch are Milkweeds or Silkpods. The white ones are of African and the yellow/red ones of American origin. Some people are allergic to the milky sap or latex. Occasionally caterpillars will be found on the Cruel Plant or Moth Vine (*Araujia sericifera*, formerly *A. hortorum*), and also on *Stapelia grandiflora*.

In New Zealand the white-flowered Milkweed is known as the Swan Plant. This is logical if you have seen the seedpods floating in a bowl of water.

This strong flying butterfly was able to naturalise itself in Australia once its food plant had become established. If all milkweeds were eliminated then the Monarch would become extinct in Australia.

Silkpod or Milkweed   HS
Asclepias curassavica

Adult male   HS
× 0.5

Swan Plant or Balloon Cotton
Gomphocarpus physocarpus HS

Swan Plant seedpod   HS
showing swan shape of seedpod

Chrysalis   HS
× 0.5

Caterpillar   HS
× 0.6

Orchard Swallowtail

Papilio aegeus

This is the second largest butterfly in the region. Male and female adults have different colouration and wing patterns. The amount of white on the wings of females also varies. Those from far north Queensland have the most white.

Caterpillars start out looking like bird droppings. There is also a spider which uses the same strategy. Mature caterpillars have two colour forms, as illustrated. Because they are commonly found on backyard citrus trees, many children are familiar with these caterpillars and their habit of poking out their osmeterium when disturbed (see p. 69).

Caterpillars pupate on their host plant, with the familiar sling. The chrysalis can be either brown or green. The colour depends on whether the background is bark or leaves.

There is a tiny black wasp which lays its eggs in the chrysalis. It is too small to penetrate a hardened chrysalis, so hangs around full-grown caterpillars waiting for their final moult.

The Orchard Swallowtail is a versatile butterfly. It is able to breed on a wide range of host plants. However, all are in the family that contains citrus. The Sandfly Bush is a small shrub with aromatic leaves and small white flowers with four petals. It can be grown from seed or cuttings.

Adult female, underside HS
× 0.5

Adult male HS
× 0.4

Caterpillar, one of the colour forms HS
× 0.5

Chrysalis HS
green × 0.5

Caterpillar, one of the colour forms HS
× 0.5

Chrysalis HS
bark camouflage
× 0.5

Sandfly Bush GL
Zieria smithii

Adult   HS
× 1.3

Adult   HS
× 0.5

Canary Beech   GL
Polyalthia nitidissima

Pale Triangle

Graphium eurypylus

This butterfly can have blue, green or yellow colour forms. In order to grow, a caterpillar must shed its skin when it gets too tight. This happens four to six times depending on the species. To get ready, caterpillars anchor their back end to a surface, their skin then splits and the new caterpillar walks out of the old skin. Often they will then eat their old skins. Caterpillars usually get a glassy look before they are ready to shed and it is important not to move them or they will lose their anchor.

The caterpillar of this butterfly makes it easy to recognize their stages. It starts off black, then changes to an orange-brown, then turns green. The chrysalis is green and even has fake veins which make it look more like a leaf.

Canary Beech is one host plant. It can become a large tree but, in dry areas, this will take a long time. It is usually grown from seed. Zig Zag Vine is another host.

This butterfly has also adapted to Custard Apple and Soursop. When there were large orchards south of Brisbane, farmers would shake the branches of their trees to disturb the hidden caterpillars. These would then poke out their osmeteria (see p. 69) which are strongly scented. From the strength of the smell the farmer would then decide whether to spray or not.

Mature caterpillar   HS
× 0.7

Young caterpillar   HS
× 1.2

Chrysalis with markings like leaf veins × 0.7   HS

Middle stage caterpillar
× 0.9   HS

Plumbago Blue

Leptotes plinius

Plumbago or Zebra Blues are one of the most reliable butterflies for a garden situation. This butterfly has benefited greatly from the popularity of the African Plumbago in landscaping. From a distance they look like small grey moths, however, up close the interesting pattern of the outside wings become visible. There will also be occasional glimpses of the lilac and blue colour of the inside wings of the male and female butterflies respectively.

The caterpillars are rarely noticed because they are so similar to the seed heads and flower buds amongst which they feed. They can be green or reddish to match the variation in colour of the seeds. In captivity the caterpillars may become cannibalistic if there is not enough food.

In the 1800's Native Plumbago grew in the Brisbane suburb of New Farm but you would need to go to Pine Mountain at Ipswich to find it in the wild today. The Native Plumbago is similar to the African one. The local one is more of a rambler along the ground, whereas the exotic is more of a bush. The seeds of both are sticky and will attach to feathers, fur and clothes to be spread far and wide. In the exotic species the sticky hairs are found only on half of the seed as shown in the photo. The native species will take root wherever the stems touch moist ground. These can be separated to make new plants. Both plants are quite robust and over time will occupy large areas if not restrained.

Native Plumbago could be a suitable replacement for the aggressive Singapore Daisy in shady places.

Adult female laying an egg   HS × 1.7

Adults, mating   HS × 1.4

Native Plumbago   GL
Plumbago zeylanica

Two caterpillars,   HS different colour forms × 1.4

Chrysalis   BM × 1.8

Plumbago (non-native)   HS
Plumbago auriculata

Adult   *JTM*
× 2.2

Purple Moonbeam

Philiris innotatus

Get up very close to this small pearly-white butterfly and you will notice the Zebra-like stripes on its legs. Males have purple upper wings and females blue. Males can often be seen perching on a leaf in a sunny and elevated spot, from which they will challenge any interlopers into their territory.

Caterpillars are flat, dimpled and resemble the colour and furry texture of the underside of the leaves of its host plant. They only eat the underside of a leaf leaving the thin upper surface intact. This results in distinctive track marks on the leaves which, if fresh, allows caterpillars to be easily located.

The Creek Sandpaper Fig is one of the most common of the three local Sandpaper Figs. It can grow into a large tree. Fruit forms not only on the ends of the branches, but also on the trunk and there can be heavy crops at times.

The fruit is almost tasty, but the fine hairs on it give it a furry texture. This deters most people though some take the extra time to rub the skin off before eating it. There is a selected form which apparently has tastier fruit.

The most common insect eating the fig tree leaves is a brown beetle. These lay their eggs in large clusters. The larvae are black and communal. They eat both sides of the leaf. Unfortunately they often defoliate trees, leaving no food for the Moonbeam.

Creek Sandpaper Fig   *GL*
Ficus coronata

The Creek Sandpaper Fig is also listed as one of the food plants of the rare Coxen's Fig Parrot.

Sandpaper Fig leaf   *HS*
showing characteristic caterpillar chew marks

Chrysalis   *HS*
× 1.9

Caterpillar   *HS*
× 1.5

Regent Skipper

Euschemon rafflesia

These are rainforest butterflies. If you are fortunate and your garden is shady, protected from wind and close to an existing population of these butterflies, you might get them to breed.

This beautiful skipper's claim to fame arises from people wanting a simple answer to the question about what the difference is between butterflies and moths. See the Moth section (p. 77) for more information.

Veiny Wilkiea is a favoured host plant and is usually found as an understorey plant in rainforest or along creeks. It grows slowly but steadily in a garden. It is usually propagated from seed.

A study of Wilkieas in the wild showed that each leaf stayed on the plant for an average of eight years when not eaten by caterpillars.

The caterpillars can feed on older leaves as well as the young ones generally preferred by other butterflies. They hide in a shelter made by sewing two leaves together and pupate in this shelter. Caterpillars need to be raised on potted plants.

Occasionally forms are found that have the yellow areas on the wings replaced with white.

Adult   *JTM*
× 1.4

Adult   *JTM*
× 0.8

Caterpillar   *HS*
× 0.7

Leaf shelter   *HS*
made by a caterpillar

Chrysalis   *JTM*
× 0.7

Veiny Wilkiea   *GL*
Wilkiea huegeliana

Adult male   HS
× 0.6

Coastal Birdwing Vine   GL
Pararistolochia praevenosa

Coastal Birdwing Vine seedpod   GL

Richmond Birdwing

Ornithoptera richmondia

This spectacular butterfly has captured the public imagination and there has been a large community effort to increase the amount of host plant available for it. Those with long memories will remember the September 1973 edition of "Wildlife in Australia Magazine" where Garry Sankowsky offered to make available the local host plant of this butterfly.

The inside top wings of the male are iridescent green and black. The lower inside wings are mostly green. The markings on the outside wings of the female are very similar to those of the inside wings. Females are larger than males.

Coastal Birdwing Vine grows mainly in the lowlands and Mountain Birdwing Vine (*Pararistolochia laheyana*) grows at higher altit-udes. Both hosts can be slow growing in a garden and require well-drained but moist soil. Extra fert-ilizer is quite beneficial. For those suburban gardens where the local plants are unsuitable, the fast growing Tagala Vine (*Aristolochia acuminata*) from North Queensland can be substituted.

Adult female   HS
× 0.4

Chrysalis   BM
× 0.7

Caterpillar   BM
× 0.5

Scarlet Jezebel

Delias argenthona

This colourful butterfly can often be seen flying around gum trees, usually too high to get a good look at it. It is looking for the mistletoe plants that its caterpillars feed on. Females lay their eggs in groups and the caterpillars feed communally. Chrysalises are a bright yellow, probably to advertise they are toxic. However, the mistletoe bird is able to eat the chrysalises and so caterpillars will often travel great distances from their food plants before they pupate. The bright reds and yellows of the Jezebel also advertise that they are toxic to birds.

A mistletoe is a plant that has no roots of its own, instead attaching itself to other plants and tapping into their fluid system. Seeds are spread by the mistletoe bird and sometimes other birds which eat the berries.

Apostle Mistletoe was given this name be-cause at least twelve different butterflies can use it as a host plant. Most of these need special ants to look after them. This mistletoe can often been seen in winter, exposed on Crepe Myrtles which have shed their leaves. It sends out runners along the branches. It will grow quite happily on Bottlebrush trees.

To grow one, obtain fresh berries and squeeze the sticky seed onto a branch that is in the sun and on a spot where the bark is thin and still green. You may need to try many times before one successfully germinates. Mistletoes usually do not kill the trees they grow on, especially where possums have access to the trees and can eat the mistletoe leaves. Isolated trees sometimes succumb.

Adult female   HS
× 1.2

Apostle Mistletoe   GL
Dendrophthoe vitellina

Caterpillars   HS
× 0.8

Chrysalis   HS
× 1.2

Mistletoe seed germinating HS
Amylotheca dictyophleba

Adult   HS
× 2.5

Native Sensitive Plant   GL
Neptunia gracilis

Small Grass-yellow

Eurema smilax

Unlike the other Grass-yellows, this one can complete its development at lower temperatures and so it is the most widely distributed of the various species in Australia. It can also build up in large numbers which then migrate to greener pastures.

One of my earliest memories of butterflies is of a constant stream of these butterflies flying past my house for what seemed like a few weeks. I wondered where they were going and where they came from.

They can be difficult to tell apart from the other Grass-yellows, especially if they don't oblige by sitting still. Small white thin eggs are laid on the host plant. The inconspicuous green caterpillars become even less conspicuous green chrysalises. These chrysalises are suspended by a silken girdle and tail attachment typical of this group of butterflies.

Native Sensitive Plant is the most interesting of the host plants of this butterfly. The native has yellow flowers while the exotic species has pink flowers. Touching the leaves of this plant results in the leaves rapidly folding up. It is quite astonishing to see a plant actually move. This doesn't stop the caterpillars eating the leaves. It is important not to over-water this plant when growing it in a garden. It is usually grown from seed.

Those people who like growing threatened species could try Edge Senna (*Senna acclinis*). It performs well in a garden in a sunny position and grows to about one and a half metres. This plant also supports the Yellow Migrant.

Edge Senna   HS
Senna acclinis

Chrysalis   HS
× 1.5

Caterpillar   HS
× 0.8

Small Green-banded Blue

Psychonotis caelius

Small Green-banded Blues are small but distinctive butterflies. They are usually easier to find in the vicinity of their host plant. Males have lilac-blue inside wings while females have white, blue and black inside wings. The green colour of the outside wings of both males and females is iridescent.

Caterpillars look like greenish slugs and are covered in fine white hairs. This makes them very hard to see against the white underside of the leaves of their host plants. Caterpillars only eat the underside of leaves. They are not attended by ants.

Soap Tree is a common tree in open forests. The tree has grey bark. It gets its name from the leaves which produce a froth when crushed and agitated in water. The chemical responsible for producing the froth is a saponin, which is poisonous to humans. Plants containing this chemical were used by the Aborigines to stupefy fish. The plant's other common name, Red Ash, is an indication of its use as a cabinet timber tree. It is not as fast growing as other popular cabinet timber trees.

Soap Tree leaves are eaten by many different insects including beetles, sawflies and moths. The caterpillars of the Indigo Flash butterfly can also breed on this tree. They start off by eating the flower buds. This tree's popularity as a food source often gives it a well-chewed look. Also when it flowers, it attracts a similarly wide variety of insects, including butterflies. This provides many snacks for insect eating birds.

To help the seeds germinate, put them in a container and pour hot water over them. Let them soak overnight before sowing.

This tree is also a suitable host for the Alphitonia Mistletoe, *Amyema conspicuum*. Several species of butterfly can breed on this mistletoe, although most of them require special ants to tend them.

White Ash (*Alphitonia petriei*) is a rainforest relative of Soap Tree. It has softer leaves and also attracts the Small Green-banded Blue. Its spreading growth habit makes it a useful shade tree for less harsh locations.

Adult   HS
× 2.3

Soap Tree   GL
Alphitonia excelsa

Caterpillar   JTM
× 2.2

Chrysalis   HS
× 1.9

Adult   HS
× 1.4

Long-leaved Matrush   GL
Lomandra longifolia

Chrysalis case, × 0.8   HS
caterpillars pupate at the base of Lomandra leaves

Splendid Ochre

Trapezites symmomus

Approximately one third of Australia's 400 or so butterflies are small, mainly brown butterflies, whose caterpillars feed largely on Lomandras, grasses, sedges and reeds. The Splendid Ochre is one of the largest of these skipper butterflies.

Caterpillars of this skipper feed on a large Lomandra, the Long-leaved Matrush. This is a widely distributed plant which comes in varieties with smaller and larger growth habits. Flowers vary from yellow to pink. Shorter forms are found in Melaleuca wetlands and the pink flowered forms are more common at higher altitudes. Some have flowers that are lemon-scented, but beware of the spines hiding in the flower spikes or you will prick your nose.

These plants, and the related Creek Matrush (*Lomandra hystrix*) which is also a host, are commonly available in nurseries and have been widely used for landscaping, particularly along the edges of highways. They are easily grown from seeds which are produced in large quantities.

The butterfly does not always lay its eggs directly on the host plant, but may lay on nearby walls, twigs or dead leaves. Caterpillars feed at night and hide during the day at the base of the plant, or in curled up leaves nearby. Distinctive V-shaped cuts in the leaves give away its presence.

Caterpillar   JTM
× 0.7

Chrysalis   JTM
× 1.1

Caterpillar, partly HS
concealed in leaf shelter

Swamp Tiger

Danaus affinis

Occasional sightings of white monarchs can frequently be attributed to this butterfly since it is a similar size and shape and the white on the wings stands out well when the butterfly is flying. It is usually common wherever its host plant grows. As a caterpillar it collects toxins from its host plants and this is why it feels safe to slowly float around.

Caterpillars are colourful. The chrysalis is usually green or pink, and hangs upside down, suspended by its rear end. The butterfly will breed in areas away from the coast as long as its host plant is present. It has arrived and bred in our inner city garden on three separate occasions over fifteen years.

Mangrove Wax-flower Vine commonly grows close to the coast, often in sight of the ocean. It is sensitive to cold weather and so is not found in places where there is winter frost.

The star shaped flowers are unusual in being greenish. The seedpods have a triangular cross section and, when they open, the seeds float away on the wind. Seeds germinate easily and pieces of the stem will put out roots when placed in water. The vine will climb up into trees and puts out long runners across the ground.

The Swamp Tiger shares this host plant with the Lesser Wanderer and the Common Crow. Reference books also state that the Blue Tiger will breed on this plant and one person has reported having seen caterpillars on this plant. To the best of our knowledge, Blue Tigers have not laid eggs and no caterpillars have developed on this plant in our garden. Any caterpillars placed on this plant did not complete their development.

By enabling Lesser Wanderers to breed in coastal areas, this plant also helps provide protection to the Laced Fritillary which is a mimic of the Lesser Wanderer.

Cynanchum ovalifolium from North Queensland is another host vine. It is recommended for the Swamp Tiger by Garry Sankowsky. It has large leaves and grows quickly. Its seeds are easy to germinate.

Adult   HS
× 1.4

Mangrove Wax-flower Vine   GL
Cynanchum carnosum

Caterpillar   HS
× 0.6

Chrysalis   HS
× 1.0

*Adult on **Bursaria spinosa** flowers   HS
× 0.6*

Flame Tree   GL
Brachychiton acerifolius

Tailed Emperor

Polyura sempronius

This is the famous "naughty" butterfly, a reputation it has achieved because it likes to drink beer. In nature it drinks sap oozing from tree trunks or juice oozing from fallen fruit and sometimes this becomes naturally fermented. Normally difficult to approach, high-flying, fast and flighty, this butterfly becomes very laid back once it has over-indulged. It then becomes possible to see the subtle colours and patterns on the wings. This photo was taken from less than a metre away.

The caterpillar is quite stunning as it has four horns on its head. Caterpillars that feed on ferny-leaved acacias usually have many stripes, giving them the appearance of a chain of small leaflets. Those that feed on larger leaves usually have two, making them less conspicuous on large leaves. The two stripes also expand slightly when disturbed, possibly functioning like eyespots to frighten birds.

The caterpillar spins a pad on a leaf which it uses as a base station. It goes out to feed and returns to the same pad. In captivity, this means it should be raised on a potted plant because, if it is given fresh leaves every day, it will spend most of its time constructing a new shelter and eat very little.

The Flame Tree is one of the more noticeable trees when covered in masses of red flowers. Hybrid cultivars with pink or lavender flowers are now available. Some trees lose all of their leaves before flowering. Luckily, the caterpillar can use silk to anchor the leaf, on which it pupates, to the stem, or in many cases it wanders off.

Mudgee wattle (*Acacia spectabilis*) is another host.

*Chrysalis   HS
× 0.7*

*Caterpillar,   HS
a colour form × 0.8*

*Caterpillar, a colour form   HS
sitting on silk pad × 0.9*

Varied Eggfly

Hypolimnas bolina

The distinctive egg-shaped patches on the males wings give this butterfly its name. He will establish and defend a territory and, once established in a garden, can take up residence for several weeks or months. He has also been known to perch on people standing within his territory. People find this an endearing behaviour, but he is only looking for a better viewing platform.

Females vary in patterns and colours. She has many different species of host plants from which to choose for egg laying. Unlike most butterflies, she seems to pick her host plants by sight as well as taste, selecting those close to the ground. Females have been observed laying eggs on watercress and clover in our garden. Both plants are unsuitable for the caterpillars. The eggs are very small and it can lay large numbers, thus ensuring that at least some will be laid on a suitable plant. The caterpillars are black with branched orange spines.

A native host plant is Love Flower which is illustrated on page 27. Illustrated on this page is the exotic weed known as *Sida retusa*, which is also utilised as a host plant. It is not recommended, unless you have the space and desire to have your garden covered to a height of about a metre. The tough stems and strong roots make it impossible to pull out by hand and the seeds are viable for at least five years. Try growing Love Flower or perhaps Karamat instead.

Adult male   HS
× 0.6

Adult   HS
× 0.7

Adult female   HS
× 0.2

Chrysalis   HS   *Caterpillar*   HS
× 0.6   × 0.6

Sida retusa, an exotic weed   HS
Sida rhombifolia

*Adult, Tisiphone abeona morrisi   HS
× 1.3*

Varied Sword-grass Brown

Tisiphone abeona

There are two subspecies of this butterfly in the region, rawnsleyi is found north of the Brisbane River and morrisi to the south.The morrisi subspecies is found in only two locations in Queensland. The Tugun bypass at Coolangatta will eliminate one of these. It is common in NSW.

Its habitat is vulnerable to fire and while the host plants are fire adapted and recover, the butterfly chrysalises and caterpillars are destroyed. These butterflies do not travel very far, so unless part of the habitat remains unburnt, the colony will not recover.

Caterpillars hide in the leaf bases of the Sawsedge, though they betray their presence by distinctive V-shaped chew marks on the leaves. A skipper caterpillar found on the same plant hides between the centre leaves which it sews together for shelter.

There are two species of Swamp Sawsedge recorded as hosts for this butterfly. One, Stocky Swamp Sawsedge (*Gahnia sieberiana*), is robust and prefers full sun. The other, Lanky Swamp Sawsedge, prefers the shade. In our region the butterfly is usually found on the latter since it grows in the shady places the butterfly prefers.

As long as the ground is not allowed to dry out, this plant is easy to grow and quite hardy. It is difficult to transplant because, in the process, it loses most of its very large root system and dries out. The seeds are also difficult to germinate but, when a batch is successful, you will get many hundreds of plants. The leaves can cause serious cuts. Do not plant where children might play.

*Lanky Swamp Sawsedge   GL
Gahnia clarkei*

*Chrysalis   HS
× 0.8*

*Caterpillar, HS
well-camouflaged*

*Caterpillar HS
× 0.4*

White-banded Plane

Phaedyma shepherdi

This butterfly looks similar to the Common Crow but its distinctive gliding style of flight gives it away. It is usually found near creeks where many of its host plants occur.

The caterpillars are cute and look like little Scotch Terriers. They chew off bits of the ends of leaves and attach them to the rest of the leaf and hide amongst the debris. They are well-camouflaged here but the pattern of chewed leaf is so distinctive that it gives them away to the informed viewer. As discovered by Bob Miller, the caterpillar possesses a small osmeterium (see p. 69) under its head. The chrysalis looks like a bit of dead twisted leaf. Sometimes it has a coppery sheen.

It was also Bob Miller who pointed out that Koda was the favoured host plant of this butterfly. Koda can grow to be a large tree and also has a tendency to sucker if the original tree is cut down. It produces masses of small scented white flowers which becomes an edible orange fruit.

It was thought that this butterfly was a mimic of the Common Crow which is toxic to birds. However, this butterfly may sometimes be toxic in its own right. The orange brown colour at the base of the outside wings is not found in the Common Crow and would draw the attention of birds. It has also been observed wetting bits of dead vegetation with its saliva and then re-imbibing the fluid, a behaviour seen in Danaid butterflies. Koda is related to plants which contain toxic alkaloids favoured by butterflies and it would be interesting to see if it also contains these toxins.

Adult, newly emerged   HS
× 1.0

Koda   GL
Ehretia acuminata

Caterpillar   HS
× 1.0

Chrysalis × 0.8   HS
resembling a dead leaf

Adult   HS
× 0.7

Adult   HS
× 1.3

Senna sophera   HS

White Migrant

Catopsilia pyranthe

Both the Yellow and Lemon Migrants have white forms which can sometimes cause confusion with this butterfly. It also looks like the introduced Cabbage White, minus the two black spots that occur on that butterfly's forewings. The easiest way to tell them apart is by identifying the plant on which the female butterfly is laying eggs. Otherwise, it will need to remain completely still before you will be able to check the finer details against a field guide.

This butterfly lays elongated white eggs on its host plants. The green, yellow and black caterpillars grow quickly and become green chrysalises that are suspended by a distinctive sling. Often the caterpillar population will build up and all the leaves will be stripped from the plants.

There are three very similar species of Senna that serve as the host for the White Migrant. The most common one is *Senna sophera*, a short open shrub. It has leaflets with pointed, not rounded, tips. The other two are *Senna barclayana* and *S. clavigera*. These three *Sennas* are differentiated by the type of gland found near the base of the leaf. They all have long cylindrical seedpods and, no matter what they are called, they all support this butterfly.

The plants are easy to grow from seed and have attractive yellow flowers. These flowers are pollinated by those bees which are able to perform the trick of buzz pollination (see p. 71). It is probably best to treat these plants as annuals in a garden.

Chrysalis   HS
× 0.8

Caterpillar   HS
× 0.8

Cabbage white, also known in Europe as the Two Spot White
Pieris rapae × 1.2   HS

Yellow Admiral

Vanessa itea

This is one of several butterflies able to utilize tree sap or fermenting fruit as well as flowersas food. Caterpillars like to spin shelters among the leaves so it may be some time before they eat enough leaves to become noticeable. In the wild they can completely defoliate patches of nettle. Caterpillars vary between black, grey, greenish and brown. The chrysalises tend to have exactly the same shades of grey as that of the dried nettle leaves.

Stinging Nettle is the usual host and can be distinguished from the European Nettle (*Urtica urens*) by its runners. The European nettle is also usually an annual. Both support the butterfly. Moistened baking soda smeared over stung areas will help lessen the pain of the inevitable stings you'll get if you grow this plant in your garden.

Occasionally female Yellow Admirals will lay their eggs on the Native Mulberry and some of the caterpillars will develop successfully.

Native Pellitory is also used as a host and does not sting. The exotic Wall Pellitory (*Parietaria judaica*), common in Sydney, should not be grown as it has been implicated in asthma reactions. The weed, Annual Copperleaf, can be mistaken for Native Pellitory. It has a small leaf, called a bract, around the tiny flowers and does not support the butterfly.

Adult   *JTM*
× 1.2

Adult   *HS*
× 0.8

Caterpillar   HS
× 0.9

Native Pellitory   GL
Parietaria debilis

Chrysalis   HS
× 0.6

Annual Copperleaf   HS
Acalypha australis

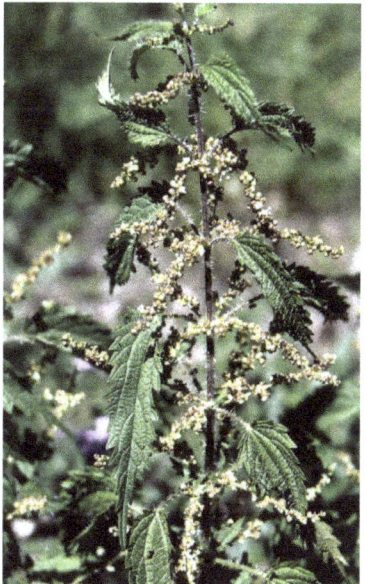

Stinging nettle   GL
Urtica incisa

Adult female BM
× 1.2

Adult female BM
× 1.2

Yellow Tulip GL
Drypetes deplanchei

Yellow Albatross

Appias paulina

Males and females of this butterfly have different markings. Males are similar to the introduced Cabbage White (see photo p. 48) and females resemble the Caper Gull.

Males are often seen engaged in the pastime of puddling. Large numbers congregate on patches of wet sand and drink lots of water. It is thought they are collecting extra minerals to be passed to the females at mating.

Freshly hatched caterpillars need young soft growth on which to feed, so expect the adults to appear after periods of wet weather which encourages this growth.

Yellow Tulip is a slow growing rainforest tree. It has a smooth grey trunk. Female trees produce red fruit. The trees are slow to grow but can eventually become large.

Adult male, showing some of life's wear and tear HS
× 1.3

Chrysalis, × 1.3 BM
top view

Chrysalis, × 1.3 BM
side view

Caterpillar BM
× 1.2

Yellow Jewel

Hypochrysops byzos

There is a specimen of this butterfly in the DPI insect collection marked Mt Gravatt 1901. This is the only trace that this butterfly once occurred in Brisbane. It still occurs further south starting at Mount Warning on the coast, and from Stanthorpe further inland. It has also been found further north at the Carnarvon Range by Geoff Monteith.

A very pretty butterfly, the colours on its outside wings are partly iridescent. The upperside wings of the male are a rich purple and those of the female each have a large orange patch. The specimens from Mount Warning are less colourful on the inside wings.

Caterpillars are particularly well disguised on the undersides of their host plant's leaves. They even remove some of the leaf hairs to make a pad into which they snugly fit when not feeding on the other leaves. They are not usually attended by ants, and frequently pupate on the plant's lower leaves.

The caterpillars feed on the leaves of many different species of Pomaderris. The Woolly Pomaderris is one of these. It is an attractive shrub with dark green felty leaves with pale undersides. Clusters of bright yellow flowers are produced once a year.

Like most Pomaderris species, they require well-drained soil. Places where they are found naturally (Mt Mee, South Ipswich and Helidon Hills) have sandstone-derived soils. They are also found on the slopes of hills like Mt Coot-tha and some of the Glasshouse Mountains where the soils are unlikely to become waterlogged.

The Rusty Pomaderris (*Pomaderris ferruginea*) is another host and has pale yellow or white flowers. The form available from nurseries is relatively hardy in a garden situation. One of the plants in our garden, which has alkaline shale-derived soil, has survived for three years, while other species have died during the humid months of January/February. Seed sometimes requires heat treatment to germinate.

Brush Kurrajong (*Commersonia fraseri*) is sometimes used as a host plant in Sydney.

Adult   HS
× 2.2

Woolly Pomaderris   GL
Pomaderris lanigera

Caterpillar   JTM
× 1.6

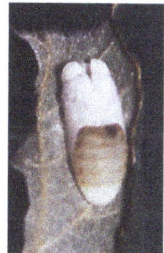

Chrysalis case HS
× 1.6

Adults, mating, wings tucked together HS
female newly emerged × 0.7

Adult   HS
× 0.7

Yellow Migrant

Catopsilia gorgophone

While this is a butterfly that migrates, it can spend winter in your garden as a chrysalis, making it possible to maintain a population for a while. Females lay their eggs over a week or two, lazily floating around the plant for the duration, and so provide a good show for their admirers. It comes in white and golden forms. Unlike the Lemon Migrant, the inner upper wings are paler than the lower wings which will help you to tell them apart.

There is a high predation rate on the caterpillars. It starts with the paper wasps which carry off the smaller caterpillars. Later the tachinid flies come and parasitise the older caterpillars. A small wasp which has pupae that hang from the host plant like small mottled ornaments is also a parasite.

One host, Climbing Senna is similar in appearance to an exotic weed, Easter Cassia (*Senna pendula* var. *glabrata*). It can be distinguished from this weed because it has flat seedpods instead of the long cylinderical ones of the exotic species. In places native plants are mistakenly being removed.

The naming of Sennas is a confusing area. However, if your plant has been named *Cassia retusa*, *Senna surattensis*, *Senna sulphurea* or *Senna gaudichaudii*, it will probably be a host for this butterfly.

European honeybees are unable to extract the pollen from these flowers. A bee needs to vibrate the flower at just the right frequency before it releases the pollen. This is called buzz pollination and many native bees, such as Teddy Bear Bees, Carpenter Bees and Blue-banded Bees (*Amegilla* spp.), are able to do it (see p.71).

Climbing Senna   GL
Senna gaudichaudii

Chrysalis HS
× 0.8

Caterpillar,   HS
with Tachinid fly egg   *× 1.0*

Getting Started with Butterfly Gardening

If you've skimmed through the preceding 48 butterflies you will have realized that there are many attractive butterflies out there just waiting to be invited to become a part of your garden. While some will be easy to attract, others will require a lot more work and perseverance. Some of the more reliable ones are mentioned below.

Many of these butterflies, the bulk of which are described more fully in the preceding pages, are those that have adapted to exotic plants related to their native host plants. Of course, as more experience is gained, the gardener can progress to the many less common, but equally rewarding, butterflies that would respond to an increase in their host plants.

In this chapter, scientific names are given where the butterfly or host plant has not been previously featured.

Orchard Swallowtail - fruity fun: Grow a lemon, orange, mandarin or grapefruit tree, and not only will you be providing yourself with some yummy fruit, but some food for the occasional caterpillar. It's a great way to get the kids away from the computer and into the real world of healthy food and the wonders of nature. You may also get the Fuscous and Dainty Swallowtails breeding on your tree.

Chequered Swallowtail   HS

Common Crow - balcony butterfly: While most people remember finding shiny, silver chrysalises on Oleander bushes, the caterpillars feed on a range of plants, one of which is the Weeping Fig. Put one in a large pot, in a semi-shaded spot. Eventually the caterpillars will come and strip away some of the foliage leaving shiny ornaments. In this way you can even have a butterfly garden on your balcony.

Chequered Swallowtail - lawn replacement: You need a large patch of the host plant, Emu Foot, to attract female Chequered Swallowtails. This is a butterfly whose beauty is frequently difficult to appreciate because it is so fast-flying. Luckily they slow down just enough for you to get a good look when they are laying eggs.

Plumbago Blue - hedge butterfly: If a hedge is what you need, don't go past the exotic Plumbago plant. The small Plumbago Blue butterfly, is almost a permanent fixture around this plant.

Speckled Line-blue - wildlife tree: This butterfly (*Catopyrops florinda*), not described in the preceding pages, is another of the cheerful, small blue butterflies. It has tiny little tails on its hind wings. Its host plant, the Native Mulberry, is a great wildlife plant. The small white berries of the female tree are attractive to a wide range of fruit-eating birds. Once the local Scaly-breasted Lorikeets discover your tree, they will regularly visit as long as it keeps fruiting. Hedge Grasshoppers (*Valanga irregularis*) also do well on this tree and may attract a Crested Hawk. Smaller insect-eating birds may also be attracted. If you're lucky the caterpillars of the beautiful Jezebel Nymph butterfly also will feed on your tree, along with the occasional Yellow Admiral.

Pale Triangle - bush tucker, yum!: The Zig Zag Vine has small but tasty, tangy orange fruits that are much sought after by connoisseurs of bush tucker. The plant can be pruned into a shrub, or left to grow naturally as a vine. It can be slow to grow in the beginning but is worth the wait. Pale Triangles can be blue, green or yellow in colour. Occasionally, you'll be lucky and have the Four-bar Swordtail caterpillars feeding on your vine as well.

Large Grass-yellow - autumn colour: While this butterfly is found throughout the year, the population peaks in March to April. This cheerful, small, bright yellow butterfly will provide a dash of welcome autumn colour to your garden. One of its host plants is the native *Breynia*, or the exotic *Breynia nivosa*. It also feeds on the Mudgee wattle, *Acacia spectabilis*, which is also one of the food sources for the spectacular Tailed Emperor, as well as Imperial Hairstreak and Moonlight Jewel (*Hypochrysops delicia*) caterpillars.

Leafwing - ground cover: Have you overdone the rainforest trees and now need a good ground cover for a moist partially shady spot? What about the very pretty Love Flower (see the Leafwing section). There are many forms of this small herb, and they will self-seed to provide a permanent ground cover if the location is suitable. The Leafwing butterfly, as its name suggests, looks like a dead leaf. You'll need a fairly large area of this plant to encourage this butterfly to lay its eggs, and then you'll be rewarded by seeing its very spectacular caterpillars. Other butterfly caterpillars including the Varied Eggfly, Blue Argus, Blue-banded Eggfly, and the Danaid Eggfly, also feed on this plant at times. The last three of these butterflies are less common in the region.

Dainty Grass-blue - frog pond: Would you like to liven up your frog pond? You could try growing a pot of Karamat in it. This swamp plant is the host for the Dainty Grass-blue butterfly, whose caterpillars eat the unripe seedpods. It is one of our smallest butterflies. Flowers only last half a day giving the pollinators, Blue-banded Bees, only a very short time to find food from this plant.

Yellow Migrant – Go for Gold: The Yellow Migrant is a medium sized butterfly with beautiful golden outside wings. Its host plant, Climbing Senna, is a good native replacement for Easter Cassia, an exotic. This plant needs to grow in full sun to be attractive to the butterfly.

Blue Tiger - Welcome stranger: Many cultures have traditions of hospitality for travellers, so why not include this travelling butterfly. Yellow Monsoon Bells are very attractive to this butterfly. In years when few of these butterflies migrate you will be able to console yourself with its pretty yellow flowers. This plant usually stops growing in winter.

From the preceding you may have realized that you are already engaged in some sort of butterfly gardening. Even those people who only grow exotics can still support some butterflies. Those people who become more interested in the plight of our local butterflies usually progress to a more native based garden.

If you are interested in a practical guide to establishing a native garden then the best place to start is the book "Grow Natives on the Gold Coast" by Graham J McDonald. Particular attention is given to the effect of soil type on planting choices. While it concentrates in detail on the Gold Coast, it is still useful for other areas of south-east Queensland and northern New South Wales that have similar soil types and climate.

Further reading: McDonald, G. (2004). *Grow Natives on the Gold Coast: a practical guide for gardeners.* Nerang : Society for Growing Australian Plants (Qld Region) Inc. Gold Coast Branch.

Guests for Dinner

While many people are making an effort to move to more native based gardens, this is not really possible for those people with little growing space who grow their own fruit and vegetables. There are some bush foods suitable for these gardens but most common food plants are exotics - some of which are host plants.

When one is a gardener it can be difficult not to have a hostile attitude to all those creepy crawlies that want to munch your favourite plants, particularly when you are expecting tasty fruit. However, most people are able to make an exception in the case of butterflies and some moths (or treat them as "flying flowers" if that makes it any easier).

As already mentioned, every butterfly was once a caterpillar, and most butterflies rely on only one species of plant or a group of related plants. This means it is unlikely that their caterpillars will gobble up every single one of the plants in your garden. They can damage young plants and they can also be a problem in orchards. This is especially the case where a monoculture of one plant can allow the

Fuscous Swallowtail   HS

build-up of large numbers of one type of butterfly. Otherwise, in these days of outsourcing just about everything, we prefer to look on caterpillars as nature's unpaid pruners.

The other reason that caterpillars don't get out of control is the balance of nature. Everything eats everything else and, in the case of butterflies, their role in life seems to be to provide food for everything else. Of course, butterflies don't necessarily approve of this role in life. One of the interesting things to observe in butterfly gardening is all the little tricks that the adult butterflies and their caterpillars get up to, to avoid being eaten. An astute observer can use this knowledge to reduce the effect of pest damage to their plants.

This brings us to the first butterfly you are likely to find in your fruit and vegetable garden. It is the Orchard Swallowtail on Citrus trees such as oranges and lemons. These trees also support two other butterflies the Fuscous Swallowtail and the Dainty Swallowtail.

Anyone growing a Custard Apple or Soursop is likely to find caterpillars of the Pale Triangle. Zig Zag Vine (*Melodorum leichhardtii*) is a native fruit in the Custard Apple family and is another host for the Pale Triangle. It is one of the tastier native fruits. The Four-barred Swordtail is an attractive butterfly whose caterpillars also feed on the leaves of this plant. It is one of the few Australian swallowtails that actually has tails.

The Blue Triangle is a butterfly that looks similar to the Pale Triangle. In suburbia, its caterpillars feed on the introduced Camphor Laurel, as a substitute for the native laurels that are its usual host plants. Its caterpillars also feed on the leaves of the Cinnamon Tree (*Cinnamomum zeylanicum*) the bark of which is turned into the spice of the same name. Small, white, spherical eggs are laid on the soft red new growth.

The Purple Moonbeam prefers the native Sandpaper Figs. However, it is also found on the European Fig which has leaves of a similar texture.

Millaa Millaa fruit   HS

Native Mulberry fruit   HS

Zig Zag Vine   HS

Millaa Millaa (*Elaeagnus triflora*) is another tasty native fruit. It's a vine with a similar sprawling habit to Bougainvillea. The caterpillars of the Indigo Flash butterflies start their lives chewing on the soft flower buds but eventually progress to the soft young leaves. If they run out of leaves these caterpillars can become cannibalistic, ensuring that at least some of them make it to adulthood. Sometimes the caterpillars are also found on Longan and Lychee flowers.

The Glasswing butterfly normally lays a batch of about forty eggs on the leaves of native passionfruit plants. It has not adapted to the exotic common Passionfruit or its larger-fruited relative, the Granadilla, but has managed to sometimes complete its life cycle on the Banana Passionfruit (*Passiflora mollissima*). Because its caterpillars are communal, it can cause a lot of defoliation on an individual plant. It has a pretty chrysalis (see page 21).

The Macadamia has several small butterflies that use it as a host. Unfortunately most of these start out eating the flower buds. One, the Bright Cornelian (*Deudorix diovis*), has a caterpillar that eats the kernel of the nut. It leaves a hole in the shell for waste disposal and plugs it with its heavily armoured rear end (which bizarrely has a smiley face on it). The other butterflies which can use Macadamia are the Common Pencilled-blue (*Candalides absimilis*), Hairy Line-blue (*Erysichton lineata*), Large Purple Line-blue (*Nacaduba berenice*), Purple Line-blue (*Prosotas dubiosa*) and Small-tailed Line-blue (*Prosotas felderi*). Considering the other moths and beetles that also feed on it, it's little wonder that it first became a commercial crop in Hawaii, far away from its native pests.

Some people who are interested in herbs grow Stinging Nettles as a medicine and vegetable (it loses its sting when cooked, but has a weird texture). Both the European and very similar native Stinging Nettle are host to the Yellow Admiral butterfly. Its caterpillars can totally defoliate a patch of nettles which, however, usually recover much faster than we would like. The caterpillars partially roll up the leaves with silken webbing that protects them from some predators.

The adult Yellow Admiral is one of a few butterflies that feed on fermenting sap and fruit. Two others are the Evening Brown and the Tailed Emperor. So, if you miss some fruit and it falls to the ground, you may find these butterflies feeding on it. When birds pecked holes in our grapes the Tailed Emperor would come and feed on them. Some people have been able to attract this adult butterfly with a bowl of mashed, overripe bananas and beer.

Sweet potato leaves can be used to hand-feed the caterpillars of the Varied Eggfly. No one has yet reported to us that they have seen the butterfly lay eggs on this plant. However, this has been recorded overseas.

The native Scrub Caper has flower buds which can be pickled in the same way as the European Caper, to which it is related. However, you are unlikely to get many flower buds if the Caper White butterflies find your plant and their caterpillars defoliate it.

The Native Mulberry is a fast growing pioneer plant if given plenty of water. The berries produced on the female plants are edible but bland, and are produced over a period of about six months. Usually the local birds will beat you to the berries. Speckled Line-blue and Jezebel Nymph butterflies lay their eggs on this plant, as occasionally will the Yellow Admiral butterfly. Caterpillars of the Varied Eggfly will accept the leaves.

Pumpkin is the most unlikely caterpillar food plant. When people run out of Milkweed leaves for their Monarch caterpillars they cut up bits of the pumpkin fruit (not the skin) and use these to feed the half-grown caterpillars. They don't grow as fast or as big but they will be able to complete their development.

As more and more exotic fruits are grown people will probably notice other butterflies using them as host plants, particularly if they are closely related to any native host plants. This can only make our gardens even more interesting places.

Rau dang is the Vietnamese name of a vegetable and translates as bitter herb. The form of this plant that grows in Australia is called Slender Carpet Weed (*Glinus oppositifolius*) and grows around the edges of billabongs and creeks. It is used as a host by the Spotted Grassblue butterfly (*Zizeeria karsandra*).

The most common butterfly in the vegetable patch is the Cabbage White butterfly (for an illustration see page 48). This butterfly comes from Europe and, as its name suggests, its caterpillars feed on cabbages and related plants. There are other moth caterpillars that also feed on cabbages. Some people grow Nasturtiums near their cabbage patch. The caterpillars can develop on this plant and some butterflies may be decoyed away from the cabbages. Optimistically there is also the possibility that you will build up a population of predators that will help protect your cabbages. Pessimistically you may also be breeding more Cabbage White butterflies.

Wild butterfly locations

Whilst it can be very satisfying to have many butterflies breeding in your own garden, the great bulk of butterflies originate in non-urban areas. Butterflies like the Plumbago Blue and the Common Crow could probably survive indefinitely in suburbia. Butterflies like those that breed on Dodder (*Cassytha* spp.) or those that rely on ants, need large natural areas to survive. To ensure that future generations continue to enjoy our local butterflies we need to ensure that these areas remain.

Aristolochia meridionalis for Clearwing Swallowtail   HS

What follows is a short guide to a very small selection of the places where butterfly plants can be found in the Brisbane area. The locations have been selected because they have either been a part of the Butterfly & Other Invertebrates Club's excursion program or projects or are a Club member's project. In naming the following few locations and groups we would like to acknowledge the great work happening in bush regeneration sites across the whole region covered.

While many other host plants, some mentioned elsewhere in this book, may also be found in these locations, the information presented here is about some special features of these locations. Unfortunately, without an identification guide, many of the plants might be difficult to find without assistance. Luckily, many of these places have associated organizations, and contact details are given at the end of the information about each location. Also, in this section, common and scientific names are used throughout.

Boondall Wetlands

The Boondall Wetlands is a Brisbane City Council reserve of over 1,000 hectares lying on the edge of Moreton Bay. The wetlands include a variety of habitats that are renowned for the diversity of birdlife. The wetlands also provide a home for many species of butterflies.

Monkey Rope (*Parsonsia straminea*) is a large vine common on the trees around the Visitors Centre. It has opposite leaves and bunches of small yellowish flowers. These flowers, though small, are a good source of nectar for many insects. Some of the local butterflies can often be seen around these flowers. It is a food plant for the caterpillars of the Common Crow butterfly. The shiny metallic chrysalis of this butterfly can sometimes be seen in the foliage.

Cressida Pipeflower (*Aristolochia meridionalis*) is a small creeper that can form an extensive groundcover when not being pruned by the caterpillars of the Clearwing Swallowtail (*Cressida cressida*). The unusual flowers are followed by ribbed seed pods which release small heart- shaped black seeds. The Clearwing Swallowtail lays small round orange eggs on the plant.

Billy Buttons (*Chrysocephalum apiculatum*) is a small wildflower with greyish leaves and yellow button-shaped flowers. It is a host plant of the Australian Painted Lady (*Vanessa kershawi*).

Grey Mangrove (*Avicennia marina*) is one of the common mangroves of Moreton Bay. It has distinctive roots, called pneumatophores, which protrude out of the mud. It is a host for two jewel butterflies, the Copper Jewel (*Hypochrysops apelles*) and the Mangrove Jewel (*Hypochrysops epicurus*). The caterpillars of these butterflies are associated with small black ants which live in borer holes in the trees. Each has its own type of ant. The distinctive marks on the leaves are formed by caterpillars' pattern of eating.

Dodder (*Cassytha filiformis*) is an unusual twining plant. It is a parasite and attaches itself to other plants with small suckers, called haustoria. The caterpillars of the Small Dusky-blue (*Candalides erinus*) come out at night to feed.

River Mangrove (*Aegiceras corniculatum*) is a shrub which has attractive, perfumed, white flowers. It is a host for the White-banded Line-blue (*Nacaduba kurava*).

Blunt-leaved Passion Vine (*Passiflora aurantia*) is a very attractive vine that is rarely seen. The large flowers start off as light pink and change to red. The fruit is eaten by Blue-tongue Lizards when it falls to the ground and becomes soft. The caterpillars of the Glasswing butterfly feed on the leaves. If they eat all the leaves they search the ground for plants of the Spade Flower (*Hybanthus stellarioides*). This small plant has flowers with a single orange petal and is also used as a host plant.

Soap Tree (*Alphitonia excelsa*) supports many different insects, one of which is the Small Green-banded Blue (*Psychonotis caelius*). The caterpillars feed on the underside of the leaves. Sometimes the caterpillars of the Indigo Flash (*Rapala varuna*) will be found feeding on the flower buds.

Tuckeroo (*Cupaniopsis anacardioides*) is popular as a street tree. This is also the case for the many varieties of small blue butterflies whose caterpillars mostly feed on the flowers and buds. The Common Pencilled-blue (*Candalides absimilis*) has a caterpillar which utilises the fresh new shoots, while the caterpillars of the Bright Cornelian (*Deudorix diovis*) feed on the seeds inside the fruit.

The Slender Rice Flower (*Pimelea linifolia*) is an attractive plant with white flowers. The caterpillars of the Yellow-spot Blue (*Candalides xanthospilos*) start by feeding on the flowers.

Samphire (*Sarcocornia quinqueflora*) is an unusual, leafless succulent which grows on the saltflats. In the past it was eaten as a salad vegetable. It is a host plant for the Saltpan Blue (*Theclinesthes sulpitius*).

Karamat (*Hygrophila angustifolia*) is another plant that has become uncommon but can still be seen in these wetlands. It has small purple flowers which last half a day and eventually produces distinctive clusters of seed pods. These are eaten by the caterpillars of the Dainty Grass-blue (*Zizula hylax*). Other butterflies which breed on this plant are the Meadow Argus (*Junonia villida*), Blue Argus (*Junonia orithya*) and the Chocolate Argus (*Junonia hedonia*).

Mangrove Milk Vine (*Cynanchum carnosum*) is the host of the Swamp Tiger (*Danaus affinis*) and sometimes also the Lesser Wanderer (*Danaus chrysippus*).

The Needle-leaf Mistletoe (*Amyema cambagei*) often goes unnoticed growing on Swamp Oak (*Casuarina glauca*) because the leaves look similar. This mistletoe is a host for two jezebels, the Black Jezebel (*Delias nigrina*) and the Scarlet Jezebel (*Delias argenthona*). As well it is also a host for the Satin Azure (*Ogyris amaryllis*) and the Purple Azure (*O. zosine*). The caterpillars of these Azures feed at night and shelter in the nests of ants during the day.

Fishbone Cassia (*Chamaecrista nomame*) grows up to a metre tall and looks like a small Cassia. The yellow flowers are followed by flat black seed pods which twist distinctively after opening. The form here, which grows amongst Blady Grass (*Imperata cylindrica*), is taller than that which grows amongst Kangaroo Grass (*Themeda triandra*) on Mt Coot-tha. The caterpillars of the No-brand Grass-yellow (*Eurema brigitta*) feed on the leaves. Seeds of this plant germinate well after fires and this is when it is usually noticed.

The Arrowhead Violet (*Viola betonicifolia*) has almost completely disappeared from Brisbane. It is a host for the Laced Fritillary (*Argyreus hyperbius*) which is a highly endangered butterfly.

Many of the Acacias, Lomandras and grasses are also butterfly host plants.

Contact: Boondall Wetlands Visitor Centre, Boondall Wetland Reserve, Gateway
    Arterial Roundabout, Boondall, 4034

Mt Coot-tha

Mt Coot-tha is a well-known Brisbane landmark. Charles McCubbin immortalised the Mt Coot-tha lookout in his book 'Australian Butterflies'. He writes about the Varied Eggfly:

Imperial Hairstreak caterpillar attended by ants, see p. 62   HS

"(*Hypolimnas bolina*) is very common in Brisbane, and my illustration shows the butterflies with their food-plant, *Sida rhombifolia*, against that splendid example of 'council baroque' which graces the summit of Mount Coot-tha."

However, most visitors are not aware that the hill is actually named after an insect, a native bee.

"There were two kinds of native honey. One called 'kabbai' was pure white and very sweet, and was found always in small, dead, hollow trees. 'Kuta' was dark honey, of a somewhat sour taste, and might be found in any kind of tree; it was much more plentiful than the other. My father gave the latter name to the Government for the hill near One-tree Hill, as in the old days that was a great place for native honey, and it has been mispronounced and spelt Coot-tha."

So wrote Constance Petrie on page 77 in her book "Tom Petrie's Reminiscences of Early Queensland". Interestingly, both species of native stingless honeybees are still known in the general area, one common and the other rare. These two species, while not originally identified are likely to be the two local native social stingless bees, *Tetragonula* (formerly *Trigona*) *carbonara* and *Austroplebeia australis*.

Another reason Mt Coot-tha is important to insects is that it is one of the places where the behaviour known as hill-topping occurs. This is the name given to the way some insects find their mates. They simply head for the nearest high hill. Think of it as a singles bar for insects!

There are many walking tracks on the hill, though you would need to be quite fit and nimble for some of them. What follows is a small selection of the butterfly host plants that you may be able to spot if you do decide to try them out.

Slender Rice Flower (*Pimelea linifolia*) occurs in the open forest. It is fire adapted and tends to disappear over time in suburbia. Its seeds are also difficult to germinate. This is a pity as it is a very attractive wildflower. Another species of Rice Flower, Pimelea latifolia, occurs in a few of the shady gullies. Both are host plants for the Yellow-spotted Blue (*Candalides xanthospilos*).

The Cressida Pipeflower (*Aristolochia meridionalis*) is a common, though usually overlooked, small vine creeping through the grass. The easiest way to find it is to closely observe any female Clearwing Swallowtails (*Cressida cressida*), as they go about laying their orange eggs. When there are lots of caterpillars most of the vines get eaten, and they become difficult to find.

Dodder (*Cassytha filiformis*) is an unusual parasitic plant which is usually found trailing through the grasses and small shrubs. Small white berries provide a welcome snack for small birds. At night, small green slug-like caterpillars of the Small Dusky-blue butterfly (*Candalides erinus*) feed on the twining stems. The small whitish blue butterflies are one of the few butterflies that are common in dry eucalypt forests. Two black spots on the upper-side of the outside wings make it easy to identify this butterfly.

Tephrosia (*Tephrosia rufula*) is a small shrub with pink, pea flowers. It is a host for the Purple Cerulean butterfly (*Jamides phaseli*). Once again, these have a small green slug-like caterpillar.

Hairy Indigo (*Indigofera hirsuta*) is a bushy plant with orange-pink pea flowers. The leaves, as its common name suggests, are slightly hairy. We were unaware that this plant grew on Mt Coot-tha until we saw its associated butterfly flying around on the ridge that is a favourite spot for skink watching. The Jewelled Grass-blue (*Freyeria putli*) is one of Australia's smallest butterflies and, when it finished sipping nectar from the Yellow Wood Sorrel (*Oxalis* spp.) flowers, it led us to a few of its host plants amongst the grasses.

Fishbone Cassia (*Chamaechrista nomame*) is a small herb with yellow flowers that resemble a small cassia. Its seeds germinate best after fire, and this is the time when the plant is most common. The green caterpillars of the No-brand Grass-yellow (*Eurema brigitta*) feed on the leaves. Sometimes the empty carcass of a caterpillar, surrounded by many tiny white cocoons, will catch your eye and lead you to this plant. This is the result of a common parasite of this butterfly, a tiny wasp.

Love Flower (*Pseuderanthemum variabile*) is a delightful small herb with flowers that vary from white to pink to purple (see the Leafwing section). Some forms are an attractive purple on the underside of their leaves. Others have attractive white patterns on the upperside. In moister areas it becomes larger and sometimes forms an extensive groundcover. Leafwing butterflies (*Doleschallia bisaltide*) lay their eggs on the flower buds and when the caterpillars hatch they eat the leaves. The spiky caterpillars grow to a large size and must sometimes travel long distances to the next plant to find enough leaves to complete their development.

Scleria mackaviensis is a small grass-like sedge with dark green leaves. It is the host of the Wide-brand Sedge-skipper (*Hesperilla crypsigramma*). There are many other skippers breeding on Mt Coot-tha and utilizing a variety of grasses, sedges and Lomandras.

Kangaroo Grass (*Themeda triandra*) is common and is one of the hosts for the Evening Brown (*Melanitis leda*) (see this section). This butterfly is the one that looks like a leaf and is often flushed out of the grass when walking along the tracks. I still remember the place on Mt Coot-tha where I first saw its two-horned green caterpillars feeding on Kangaroo Grass. The caterpillars of the Orange Ringlet (*Hypocysta adiante*) are also said to feed on this grass but neither of us have ever seen its caterpillars in the wild, probably because its caterpillars feed at night.

Monkey Rope (*Parsonsia straminea*) can grow into a large vine. It has opposite leaves and bunches of small, yellow flowers. These flowers are an important nectar source for a large variety of insects such as beetles, wasps, bees etc. Common Crow (*Euploea core*) caterpillars feed on the leaves of this vine, the closely related Brisbane Parsonsia (*Parsonia brisbanensis*) which has white flowers, and also the Narrow-leaved Milk Vine (*Marsdenia fraseri*). All three vines grow here.

At the right time of the year the Fringed Heath-blue (*Neolucia agricola*) can be seen flying around its host plant *Pultenaea microphylla*. The caterpillars feed on the flower buds of their host plant. The butterfly lays its eggs on the plant and they must survive there until the next years' flowers emerge.

Mt Coot-tha is also home to many different species of native ants and some of these are vital protectors of some types of butterfly caterpillars. The Fiery Jewel (*Hypochrysops ignitus*) and the Imperial Hairstreak (*Jalmenus evagoras*) are two whose associated ants can be found there. The caterpillars feed on a wide range of plants including wattles (*Acacia* spp.) as long as the ants are present. The ant that looks after the Fiery Jewel is called the Coconut Ant (*Papyrius* sp.) because it smells of coconut. The ant that looks after the Imperial Hairstreak is the Kropotkin Ant (*Iridomyrmex* sp.).

Rusty Pomaderris (*Pomaderris ferruginea*) was recorded at the base of Mt Coot-tha in the 1980s. The place is now a typical suburban street. The Yellow Jewel (*Hypochrysops byzos*) whose caterpillars feed on the plant was last recorded in Brisbane at Mt Gravatt in 1901. A few plants still survive precariously on the lower slopes of Mt Coot-tha.

Another plant that has long disappeared from the Mt Coot-tha area is the Arrowhead Violet (*Viola betonicifolia*). Herbarium records show it at One Tree Hill in 1887 and 1914. The endangered Laced Fritillary butterfly (*Argyreus hyperbius*) whose caterpillars feed on this violet was recorded at nearby Indooroopilly in 1916.

It is sad to think of what has been lost from Mt Coot-tha, but there are still many plants and animals which are not only surviving but thriving. Large areas of bushland are especially important for those species that are unable to survive in suburbia, such as fire adapted plants like the Slender Rice Flower, plants with unusual habits like Dodder, or many species of unusual ants. The great variety of invertebrates also provide food for other small animals, and Mt Coot-tha is quite rich in many species of lizards not found in suburbia.

Mt Coot-tha is also home to Brisbane's TV transmitter towers. So, next time you're at home watching TV, let your thoughts travel back along the signal to Mt Coot-tha and wander over the mountain like the butterflies that still live there. Your brain will thank you for it.

Contact: The Hut Environmental and Community Association Inc. (THECA), 89 Fleming Rd., Chapel Hill, QLD 4069

Stanley River Park

Stanley River Park is a park of 6,750 square metres on the banks of the Stanley River located close to where the highway crosses the river at Peachester. It was once an overnight camp for bullock teams.

The remnant rainforest along the river contains some very old Coastal Birdwing Vines (*Pararistolochia praevenosa*). The Wildlife Preservation Society of Queensland and

Barung Landcare, with the local community, have been responsible for removing weeds, extending the rainforest section with extra trees and understorey plants, and planting an extra 240 Coastal Birdwing Vines. This project was assisted by a grant from the Natural Heritage Trust (NHT) in 1997.

Richmond Birdwing butterflies can be seen there every year along with, occasionally, their caterpillars. The preservation and enhancement of this important Richmond Birdwing breeding site is a credit to Jill Chamberlain (Honorary Secretary of the Caloundra Branch of WPSQ at the time) and all the other members of the community who were involved.

The NHT grant included enhancement of the site for other fauna and, indeed, the rehabilitation of the site has also benefited another butterfly, the Wonder Brown (*Heteronympha mirifica*). With this butterfly the sexes are so different that one could be forgiven for thinking they are different species. The caterpillars feed on a Beard Grass (*Oplismenus* sp.), a creeping grass that grows well in moist shady places. The males and females also emerge at different times so you will need to be lucky to see both in one visit.

Sadly, the endangered Laced Fritillary butterfly (*Argyreus hyperbius*), which was recorded very close to this park in 1977, has not been recorded here again.

Contact: Wildlife Preservation Society of Queensland, 95
     William St., Brisbane, QLD 4000

Richmond Birdwing
female   HS

Yoorala Street Revegetation Project, Enoggera Creek, The Gap

Vera and Fred Moffett have spent many years helping to regenerate a section of the Enoggera Creek. Starting at the rotunda in Corramulling Park, at the end of Yoorala St, The Gap, a path follows the creek for some distance. It passes a pony club field and eventually ends, upstream, in a small park. Following the creek further upstream leads to the Enoggera Reservoir and the start of Brisbane Forest Park.

The project is part of a much larger endeavour covering the Enoggera Creek catchment that was initiated by Save Our Waterways Now Inc. (SOWN). Projects in this catchment cover some forty-eight kilometres of creek banks and hundreds of kilometers of dry gullies and feeder creeks. This area was divided up into 94 manageable planning units that could be maintained in an on-going manner by volunteers and team leaders. Highlights from the Yoorala St section follow.

Bolwarra (*Eupomatia laurina*), a host for the Eastern Dusk-flat (*Chaetocneme beata*), grows along the creek. These caterpillars cut out sections of the leaves and fold them over to make shelters (see photo page 17).

The Creek Sandpaper Fig (*Ficus coronata*) is a host of the Purple Moonbeam butterfly (*Philiris innotatus*). These caterpillars leave distinctive feeding marks on the leaves that show where they have been (see photo page 36). The adult males will take up a position on the end of a sunny branch from where they can chase off any rivals. The fruit of this tree is probably eaten by the large Moggills (Water Dragons) frequenting the edge of the creek.

The Black Bean tree (*Castanospermum australe*) produces very large toxic seeds. The bright red and orange flowers are very showy and attract Lorikeets by day and Fruit Bats by night. The caterpillars of the Common Pencilled-blue (*Candalides absimilis*) can be found feeding on the fresh young leaves.

Native Wisteria (*Callerya megasperma*) can be found climbing high into the canopy of the trees. If any of the leaves are growing near ground level, you may find the rolled up shelters of the Narrow-banded Awl (*Hasora khoda*).

As its name suggests Creek Matrush (*Lomandra hystrix*) is found all along the creek. Often you will see the distinctive V-shaped notches on the leaves made by the caterpillars of the Splendid Ochre (*Trapezites symmomus*). These caterpillars hide during the day at the base of the plant.

At one point along the path there is a large multi-trunked Socketwood Tree (*Daphnandra* sp.). This tree is more often found at higher altitudes. However, this shows how trees with bird-dispersed fruit can turn up naturally in unusual places. This tree is one of the host plants of Macleay's Swallowtail (*Graphium macleayanus*).

Speckled Line-blue   HS

Amongst the granite boulders that picturesquely line the creek, you will find plants of the Love Flower (*Pseuderanthemum variabile*). The caterpillars of the Leafwing butterfly (*Doleschallia bisaltide*) hide on the underside of any leaves they haven't already eaten.

Small sandy patches on the edge of the creek will sometimes attract butterflies to come and drink. Some butterflies make a habit of this "puddling" behaviour .

This bush regeneration group has resisted the temptation to "tidy up" and many dead logs and branches have been left on site. These provide essential homes for many small invertebrates and other creatures usually too small to attract attention.

Further reading: Horton, H. ed. (2002). *A Brisbane Bushland: the history and natural history of Enoggera Reservoir and its environs.* Brisbane, Queensland Naturalists' Club Inc.

Contact: Save Our Waterways Now Inc. (SOWN), 477 Waterworks Rd., Ashgrove West, QLD 4060

White's Hill Reserve & the Bulimba Creek Catchment

The White's Hill Reserve lies within the catchment of Bulimba Creek in Brisbane. Eucalypt forest at the top of the hill gradually transitions to become remnant rainforest at the bottom. The rainforest was part of Sankeys Scrub, a favourite site for visits by the Field Naturalists section of the Royal Society in the late 1800's.

On the slopes of White's Hill can be found Smooth Tick Trefoil (*Desmodium heterocarpon*). This legume is host for the Orange-tipped Pea-blue (*Everes lacturnus*). When this plant produces seed it becomes food for a tiny weevil. In turn these weevils are parasitised by small wasps and also small flies. All this on just one small plant.

In a few places the Pointy-leaved Passion Vine (*Passiflora herbertiana*) can be found. Its large white flowers immediately distinguish it from the similar looking but exotic Corky Passion Vine (*Passiflora suberosa*). Both these plants are hosts for the Glasswing butterfly (*Acraea andromacha*).

Many of the other plants of the open forest are similar to those found on Mt Coot-tha. Slender Rice Flower (*Pimelea linifolia*), Breynia (*Breynia oblongifolia*), Hairy Indigo (*Indigofera hirsuta*) and Soap Tree (*Alphitonia excelsa*) to name a few.

In Sankeys Scrub, down along the creek line, a few Veiny Wilkieas (*Wilkiea huegeliana*) can still be found. In the late 1800's Milais Culpin collected Regent Skippers (*Euschemon rafflesia*) here, but now there are too few plants to support a viable population.

Native Mulberry (*Pipturus argenteus*) can still be found and, together with Poison Peach (*Trema tomentosa*), supports Speckled Line-blues (*Catopyrops florinda*).

There are two species of Caper plants here, *Capparis arborea* and *Capparis sarmentosa*, which support several of the Caper butterflies at various times.

Yurol or Supplejack (*Flagellaria indica*) looks a bit like bamboo as it climbs into the canopy. It is a host of the Southern Large Darter (*Telicota anisodesma*).

The Bulimba Catchment has other interesting remnants of original vegetation. For instance, Runcorn Wetlands is the home of one of Australia's smallest crayfish (*Tenuibranchiurus glypticus*), its largest dragonflies (*Petalura litorea*), and the Mountain Katydid (*Acripeza reticulata*). These last two were photographed by Peter Chew and can be viewed on his website.

Contact: Whites Hill-Pine Mountain Community Group Inc. PO Box 5, Carina, QLD 4152
   Bulimba Creek Catchment Coordinating Committee (B4C), PO Box 5, Carina, QLD 4152

Cameron's Scrub and Sapling Pocket, Ipswich

This locality preserves rare examples of softwood scrub and riparian rainforest in southeast Queensland. A large proportion is privately owned. Two significant portions are preserved as reserves. Sapling Pocket Nature Refuge is managed by the Queensland Parks and Wildlife Service (QPWS). Kholo Enviroplan (Cameron's Scrub) Reserve is managed by the Ipswich City Council. The City Council is also co-operating with local landowners to preserve this forest type on adjoining private land. Greening Australia volunteers are working with QPWS to regenerate a part of the Sapling Pocket Refuge that is being threatened by weeds. There is no visitor infrastructure. The areas are managed more as scientific reserves. Special arrangements are needed to visit these locations.

The Butterfly and Other Invertebrates Club has had several excursions to the Council Reserve with the permission of the Council. Many butterflies were recorded and details were passed to the Council.

Climbing Senna (*Senna gaudichaudii*), a host for the Yellow Migrant (*Catopsilia gorgo-phone*) has been found in the scrub, along with Lime Berry (*Micromelum minutum*), host for the Orchard Swallowtail (*Papilio aegeus*) and the Fuscous Swallowtail (*Papilio fuscus*). Zig Zag Vine (*Melodorum leichhardtii*), host for the Pale Triangle (*Graphium eurypylus*) and the Four-barred Swordtail (*Protographium leosthenes*) has also been found. Caterpillars of both these butterflies were present on one of the excursions.

The Ornate Dusk-flat (*Chaetocneme denitza*) was observed resting on the underside of a leaf. Its host plant at this location is not known.

Numerous Corky Milk Vines (*Secamone elliptica*) grow throughout the scrub. Its distinctive corky bark is easily recognized on the older, larger plants. This location is an important breeding site for the Blue tiger (*Tirumala hamata*).

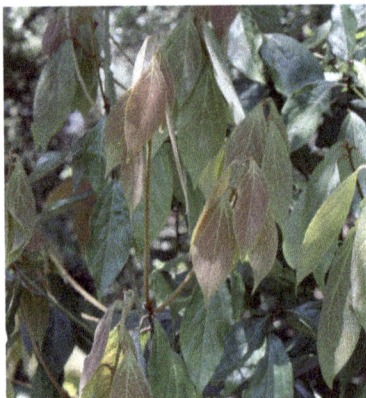

Occasionally small whitish "butterflies" were observed. A closer look revealed that these were not butterflies but day-flying lacewings. The species was identified as a Lizard's Head Lacewing (*Psychopsis coelivaga*). It takes its name from the resemblance of the pattern of the resting wings to a lizard's head. No doubt there are many other fascinating invertebrates waiting to be discovered.

Contact: Ipswich City Council
Queensland Parks and Wildlife Service, Southern Regional Office, 55 Priors Pocket Rd., Moggill, QLD
Greening Australia Queensland (Inc.),
333 Bennetts Rd., Norman Park, QLD 4170

*White Bolly Gum (**Neolitsea dealbata**)*
a host for Eastern Dusk-flat p. 67   HS

Conondale Range

About a hundred kilometres north of Brisbane, in the Sunshine Coast hinterland, lies the Conondale Range. An extensive area of eucalypt forest and rainforest, the area includes forest reserves and the Conondale National Park.

It is an important refuge for many rare animals, birds and plants. Its large variety of plants supports a wide diversity of butterfly species, far too many to list here. The Range lies in an interesting overlap area where northern tropical and southern temperate species intermingle.

The Richmond Birdwing (*Ornithoptera richmondia*) lives here. It belongs to a large group of mainly tropical butterflies. Equally at home is Banks' Brown (*Heteronympha banksii*), belonging to a mainly southern group of butterflies. A purple sheen on wings of the Bank's Brown serves to distinguish it from others of its group. Its host plant in the Conondales has not been documented yet, but is probably a grass or sedge.

Regent Skippers (*Euschemon rafflesia*), Macleay's Swallowtails (*Graphium macleayanus*) and Four-barred Swordtails (*Protographium leosthenes*) also breed here.

Bouloumba Creek is a place visited by many people and, according to local oral tradition, its name means place of white butterflies. Indeed there are places on the creek where many butterflies gather for their mysterious ritual of puddling. Host plants for Pearl Whites (*Elodina parthia, E. padusa, E. angulipennis, E. queenslandica*) and White Migrant (*Catopsilia pyranthe*) butterflies grow in the area, and so this certainly is an appropriate name.

The Woodford Folk Festival site is at the base of the Conondale Ranges. The part of the watershed it covers drains into the Stanley River and is close to the Stanley River Park. The site backs onto State Forest, so has great access to natural habitat for many species of butterflies and other invertebrates. Revegetation work on the site has been extensive and has included significant plantings of host plants for the Richmond Birdwing, Regent Skipper, White-banded Plane and Laced Fritillary.

A Butterfly Walk between the Ticket Office and the Welcome Gate was established by Des Ritchie. This walk features the host plants of over fifty local butterflies and, during the festival, photos of these butterflies are positioned on or near their host plants. If you are interested, the less well-known tree planting weekend / Environment Festival, held on the Labour Day long week-end each year in May, is a good time to become involved with this work.

Further reading: Conondale Range Committee (2004). *Walking on the Wilder Side ... in the Conondales.* The Committee. Contact: The Conondale Range Committee, PO Box 150, Kenilworth, QLD 4574

Palmwoods Arts and Crafts Group (2001). *Wings over the Sunshine Coast: Naturalists and Artists describe our Birds and Butterflies.* The Group. Contact: Palmwoods Arts and Crafts Group Inc. PO Box 227, Palmwoods, QLD 4555

Contact for Woodford Folk Festival: Internet: www.woodfordfolkfestival.com

Eprapah The Scout Environmental Education Centre

The site comprises 39 hectares at Victoria Point and was purchased in 1928 by the Scout Association. First used as a Leader Training Centre, it was reserved as an Environmental Training Centre in 1973.

An endangered species, the Mangrove Ant-blue (*Acrodipsas illidgei*), better known locally as the Illidge's Ant-blue, has been recorded at nearby Redland Bay and possibly occurs on this site. The caterpillars live inside the nests of small black ants and feed on their larvae and pupae. These ants (*Crematogaster* sp.) nest in hollow, dead branches of the Grey Mangrove (*Avicennia marina*) and these mangroves occur on the site. However, near Maryborough, less than 2% of ants nests showed any sign of the caterpillars and a similar ratio would be expected at this site.

The Eastern Dusk-flat (*Chaetocneme beata*) occurs on site. Here it breeds on the White Bolly Gum (*Neolitsea dealbata*).

Murrogun (*Cryptocarya microneura*) grows at this location. It is used as a host plant by the Blue Triangle (*Graphium sarpedon*).

There are several walking tracks and, in April 2004, a Green Corps team completed the design and construction of a butterfly garden, adding this attraction to the Senses Trail. Tours of the site can be arranged for a small charge.

Contact: Friends of Eprapah Scout Fellowship, cnr. Cleveland – Redland Bay Rds and Colburn Ave., Victoria Point. 4165

Observing Nature

Most people are content to just drive their cars around to get from A to B. A small proportion like to know how they work, to know what lies under the bonnet. A similar situation exists with butterflies. Some people are happy to just grow the plants and watch the butterflies floating around. Others would like to know the details of what is happening in their own little urban ecosystems. If you are one of these people this section is for you.

In this chapter scientific names are included where the species has not been featured in the earlier section of this book.

Don't Eat Me – the Plant's Point of View

Caterpillars grow by eating plants. However, the plants don't always co-operate. Some plants have adapted to make chemicals that poison caterpillars. That's why most caterpillars stick to a single type of plant or similar plants. Their digestive systems are tuned into the various chemicals in the plant and are able to neutralize them.

Once a species of butterfly has managed to defeat the chemical defence, some go one step further. They collect the toxins, so that anything which eats them becomes poisoned. Some plants retaliate by increasing the amount of toxin they produce. One species of native pipeflower, Tagala Vine (*Aristolochia acuminata*), that we observed, directed extra toxin to the spots on leaves where eggs were laid. The newly emerged caterpillars quickly died. The butterfly's solution to this is simple. It does not lay all its eggs directly on its host plant but lays some close to it. This is why you sometimes see Birdwing butterflies seemingly laying on the wrong plants.

Another interesting defence that some plants have is the equivalent of a burglar alarm. When the saliva of a caterpillar makes contact with a cut leaf, certain chemicals are released which are detected by the wasps that hunt caterpillars. The wasps are attracted to the plants and start searching for the caterpillars. This mechanism has been well studied in commercial plants such as cotton. Incidentally, it was discovered that this mechanism was being accidentally bred out of modern varieties of cotton, making them more susceptible to pests. With invertebrate research not well-funded, except when an animal is a pest, it is hard to find literature on this topic. My observations in my garden are that some of the plants with chewed leaves frequently have more wasps than usual flying around them.

Plants are not usually thought of as moving much, but some do make substantial use of this. The topic was studied extensively by Charles Darwin. By the way, his 593 page book on the subject, *"The Power of Movement in Plants"* is available on the Internet.

Paper daisies will close their flowers when it rains. Others such as Cassia spp. and Oxalis spp. will fold their leaves at night. The Native Sensitive Plant is one plant that has taken movement to extremes. When the plant is touched the leaves all fold together within a few seconds. When this happens the plant does not look like a bountiful meal anymore and any creature on it can't hide amongst the leaves and becomes dangerously exposed to predators. This, however, has not stopped the Small Grass-yellow from making this plant one of its hosts.

A further defence involves domatia, which are small swellings found on the underside of leaves that provide homes for mites. Some of the mites using domatia are predatory and eat other sap-sucking mites while others graze on the algae which grow on leaves. This is a good return to the plant for providing board and lodging.

Don't Eat Me – the Butterfly's Point of View

Just as many things try to eat plants, there are many predators of caterpillars and butterflies. It seems that their role is to be food for everything else. However, this fate is not accepted willingly.

Birds are significant predators of butterflies. The Orchard Swallowtail caterpillar, along with some other species of Swallowtail, has a novel approach. When small, it looks like a bird dropping. As it gets too large for this disguise to work, it has another trick. When it is disturbed, it shoots out an osmeterium (plural osmeteria) from its head. This comprises two filaments that are joined at the base, that resemble a snakes forked tongue. It emits a strong smell.

The Evening Brown has a simple solution. It spends the day sitting still looking like a leaf. It only starts to fly about at dusk when the day-flying birds have become inactive.

The Indigo Flash has hindwings with thin tails and a spot. This makes it difficult to tell which is the front or back end of the animal. When it lands it slides its wings up and down against each other. This action has the effect of making the fake antenna wobble a bit and drawing attention to it. Several little blue and grey butterflies have these little eyespots and little tails. They must work reasonably well judging by the number of older butterflies that can be observed with little bits missing from their wings at these points. Other butterflies have much larger eyespots which function to startle birds, when a butterfly suddenly opens its wings.

A very successful strategy involves those caterpillars that actively collect toxins from their host plants. Some of these try to collect even more toxins from other plants when they become adults. Butterflies such as the Lesser Wanderer, Blue Tiger and Common Crow will often be seen on Blue Heliotrope plants (*Heliotropium amplexicaule*) collecting pyrolizidine alkaloids. Not only do these taste unpleasant, but, according to Miriam Rothschild, a famous naturalist, they have a memory enhancing effect, so the unpleasant experience is better remembered.

The Cabbage White butterfly, one of the most researched species in the world, has become so dependent on the toxin it collects from its host plants in the Mustard family, that it tastes a potential host plant for the chemical before it decides to lay an egg. If you look closely at the caterpillar you will see that it is covered with many fine projections where the chemical accumulates. Ants, a frequent predator of the young caterpillars of some species, find it difficult to attack these caterpillars. The chemical is related to mustard gas. This chemical does not work on all the enemies of the butterfly, so it still needs to fly quickly, and its caterpillars are green and try to be inconspicuous.

Many of the butterflies that are toxic advertise this fact with bright colours so that birds recognize them easily. A bird may eat one of them, but if they get sick, all the other ones with that and similar colouration are left alone. These butterflies often have red or orange colours that birds see well. They also often have a leisurely floating flight pattern. The Glasswing, the Clearwing Swallowtail and the Monarch are good examples of this. Compare their flight with, for example, the fast and nervous flight of the non-toxic Blue Triangle.

Some butterflies that don't collect toxins try to look like butterflies that are toxic. The female non-toxic Danaid Eggfly (*Hypolimnas misippus*) looks like a Lesser Wanderer which is poisonous, the Jezebel Nymph looks like the Black Jezebel in the southern part of its range, and like the Scarlet Jezebel in the more northern areas.

Another concern for butterflies are the flies and wasps that lay their eggs on their caterpillars. There are many types of these parasites, but the ones that most people are familiar with are the Tachinid Flies. These flies are the ones responsible for the chrysalises of the Common Crow turning black and no butterfly emerging. Often a thin thread hangs from the chrysalis to mark the place where the maggot eventually emerged. You can see a photo of one of these flies stalking a caterpillar of the Clearwing Swallowtail (see p. 13).

The photo of the Yellow Migrant caterpillar (see p. 52), shows one of the small white eggs of a Tachinid Fly, indicating that this caterpillar was doomed. Compare this with the caterpillar of the White-banded Plane (see p. 47). It has two white spots, at the rear end, which resemble those of a Tachinid Fly. Too many eggs on one caterpillar would mean that there would not be enough food for any of the flies to reach adulthood. Perhaps this is a way of discouraging a Tachinid Fly, by making it think that this caterpillar was already taken. This does not work every time because I have seen many of these caterpillars which had still been parasitized.

The caterpillars of the Jezebel Nymph have a different strategy. These caterpillars are gregarious and, in their early stages, form a circle when they are resting (see the photo, p. 24). The formation of these young caterpillars look spider-like and, therefore, appears to be a threat. The pattern makes it very difficult for a Tachinid Fly to approach the side of any caterpillar to attach its eggs. With a large number of caterpillars there is a good chance that some would escape even if the fly was successful.

It is no easy task for a Tachinid Fly to find its victim. Caterpillars tend to hide and some only eat in short bursts. However, caterpillars have one weakness. Wherever they go they put down a silken line. This not only helps them find their way around, but acts as a lifeline if they happen to fall from a plant. One type of Tachinid Fly has a shuffling kind of walk where it seems to drag its feet along the leaves and branches in order to contact part of the caterpillars' lifelines (or should we now say deathlines). If such a lifeline is detected, the fly knows there is probably a caterpillar nearby. The search then begins in earnest to find the caterpillar. I once saw one of these flies land on a Milkweed plant and spend a lot of time looking for the caterpillar. The caterpillar was one that often left its plant, and this time it was lucky to be away when the fly called.

I also suspect that some Tachinid Flies are aware when plants are being chewed by caterpillars. One of my potted plants was being chewed by a moth caterpillar that fed only at night and stayed concealed during the day. At a time when there had been a build up of the Tachinid Fly population, this plant attracted many flies and they spent a lot of time searching it without success. I recognized one of the species as being similar to the fly known to lays its eggs on the host plant rather than on the caterpillars themselves. This is a good strategy for the fly which is active by day to get those caterpillars that only come out at night. This Tachinid Fly is the one responsible for parasitising caterpillars raised indoors behind fly-screens but fed on leaves brought in from outside. Ross Kendall, from Butterfly Encounters, treats his leaves with a 0.4% liquid chlorine (Sodium hypochlorite) solution for ten to fifteen minutes before rinsing them off with plenty of fresh water. This eliminates most Tachinid Fly eggs.

Caterpillars produce a lot of frass and its odours attract the attention of predators. In the USA, Paper Wasps (*Polistes* spp.) have been shown to use this to track down caterpillars. Shelter-building caterpillars, because of their fixed location, are particularly at risk. Some have evolved a mechanism to discharge their frass at high speed. The Silver-spotted Skipper (*Epargyreus clarus*) also from the USA, shoots its pellets an average of 19 times its body length. This makes it difficult for the wasps to find the caterpillars.

There are many creatures that eat butterfly eggs, from tiny wasps that develop completely within an egg, to spiders, ants, etc. One butterfly, the Bordered Rustic, tries to give it eggs some protection by laying them directly on old spider webs.

There is a diversity of other creatures that prey on caterpillars such as assassin bugs, spiders, even the flatworms or planarians that usually feed on earthworms. Some of the most common are the wasps that build those papery nests. There are many different kinds of these but their main food is small caterpillars. Those people who garden organically often try to provide conditions to encourage these creatures to protect their food crops.

Pollination

Plants must replace themselves and observing the different types of flowers, their colours, shapes, scents, etc. that make this possible is quite interesting. Bees are the most well-known pollinators of flowers. There are over 1,500 species of native bees. If you grow Love Flowers you will probably see the Blue-banded Bee (*Amegilla* spp.) busily visiting its flowers. The Red-bodied Bee (*Chalicodoma* sp.) will visit flowers of Rattle-pods (*Crotalaria* spp). In a herb garden, a large bush of perennial Basil will attract Leaf-cutter Bees (*Megachile* spp.) to its nectar. Large Carpenter Bees (*Xylocarpa* sp.) and small Teddy Bear Bees (*Amegilla* sp.) will visit the flowers of Sennas. Senna flowers will only release their pollen when they are vibrated at the right frequency. This means only those lucky bees able to buzz pollinate will have access to the valuable pollen.

Hives of a small stingless native bees (*Tetragonula carbonara*) often feature in wildlife gardens. These bees pollinate a wide range of plants. One they find particularly attractive is Old Man Salt-bush (*Atriplex nummularia*). It is the host plant of the Saltbush Blue (*Theclinesthes serpentata*).

While Sennas prefer bees, the Apostle Mistletoe (*Dendrophthoe vitellina*) prefers honeyeaters to do its pollination. In fact, it is so adamant about this that it does not normally open its flowers until the ends have been tapped by the beak of a honeyeater. If you have access to this mistletoe in flower you can tap a flower that seems mature and see how it opens up.

Some plants have given up on insects and birds altogether, and rely on the wind to transfer their pollen. This way they can save on giving out all that free nectar. Stinging nettles do this, as does a little native Plantain (*Plantago debilis*), one of the hosts of the Meadow Argus. The male Native Mulberry also does this and sometimes you can see a tiny puff of yellow as the flower releases its pollen. The female flowers have a feathery look which makes it easier to contact drifting pollen.

Butterflies are also able to pollinate many flowers and most butterfly gardens contain some plants that are especially attractive to butterflies. The Australian Painted Lady butterfly (*Vanessa kershawi*) will be seen to get its nectar from the flowers of the Paper Daisy (*Xerochrysum bracteatum*) that its caterpillars feed on. The Jewelled Grass-blue (*Freyeria putli*) will visit the flowers of the Yellow Wood Sorrel (*Oxalis* sp.) frequently growing near its host plants. Plants with clusters of small tubular flowers are most attractive to butterflies. The best known of these are the exotic Buddleias and the native Lime Berry (*Micromelum minutum*).

Various plants are not fussy about what pollinates them and all sorts of insects and sometimes even birds and bats turn up when they flower. The flowers of the Soap Tree usually have a hum of many types of insects, as will the small but nectar-laden flowers of the Monkey Rope vine. These plants are some of the most interesting nectar plants because you never know what will turn up next.

When flowers have an odour similar to rotting fruit or decomposing meat, they are usually pollinated by flies. The tiny flowers of the Lollygobble Vine (*Salacia chinensis*) from North

Queensland smell of rotting fruit and are pollinated by a small black fly similar to a fruit fly. More interesting yet are the small maroon spots on the lower petal of a Love Flower. These attract Hover Flies that seem to be tasting them with their feeding tube, called a proboscis.

The weirdest flower is that of the Birdwing Vine. It attracts tiny midges which climb down into the bulb at the base of the flower. Tiny hairs close the neck of the flower and keep the midges locked in overnight. They are then released the next day covered in pollen ready to enter the next flower.

A most perplexing flower is that of the Silkpod or Milkweed. The first challenge is to find where the pollen is. The next is to work out where it has to go and then how all this is to be accomplished. The flower of the Silkpod has its pollen in discrete bundles similar to Orchids, but in this case they come in pairs which are yoked together by a saddle. These bundles are supposed to become attached to the legs of visiting insects that have come to sip nectar. The pollen then gets transferred to the next flower where it fits neatly into another part of the flower. This seems unnecessarily complicated but it must work because there are always plenty of seeds.

The most complicated pollination is that of the humble fig. The "fruit" is basically an inside out Mulberry composed of what were once many tiny flowers. A hole at the end of the receptacle allows the pollinator, a tiny wasp, to get in and out. This wasp completes its lifecycle inside the receptacle, which will become the fruit. There is a complicated process which ensures that some wasps from one receptacle go to another to enable crosspollination. This system must support a huge population of wasps, because large old fig trees often have numerous swallows flying around them when the fruit is forming. They are likely to be feeding on these tiny wasps.

Ants

When you first see them, it is hard to imagine that the large number of ants, which are swarming all over the caterpillars of the Imperial Hairstreak are up to any good (see p. 22). That many ants would surely gobble up the hapless caterpillars in no time at all. Contrary to first impressions, they are, in fact, guarding the caterpillars against attack. In return the ants receive various nutritious, amino acid containing secretions.

That this cooperation exists seems to be a violation of the laws of natural selection. The struggle for survival pits animal against animal resulting in the survival of the fittest, the socalled "law of the jungle". What a surprise to find ants and caterpillars cooperating. This is not unique. There are many species of butterflies associated with many species of ants. While Darwin himself recognized that natural selection could favour cooperative behaviour in certain circumstances, it was the Russian Prince Peter Kropotkin's 1902 classic work titled "Mutual Aid" which really opened up this field. Indeed, this cooperative behaviour is now called mutualism by scientists.

Sometimes plants try to cut out the middleman, that is the caterpillar, and provide their own nutritious secretions directly to the ants. They do this with glands called nectaries which are usually found at the base of leaves. Wattles often have these glands along with most Sennas.

The glands on the Macaranga (*Macaranga tanarius*) have been shown to produce a secretion containing six soluble sugars and up to eight amino acids. When the leaves were artificially damaged there was a significant increase in the production of this nectar for the next three days. This would concentrate the ants where they would most be needed for the plant's protection. For cotton plants a twelve-fold increase in nectar production by leaves damaged by moth caterpillars was recorded.

Ants sometimes tend aphids and scale insects feeding on plants. Scale insects can be damaging not only because they take sap but also because they can cover the leaves and reduce their photosynthesis and, therefore, reduce the flow of sap. The Shiny-leaved Canthium (*Canthium odoratum*) has reached a compromise with the ants. The plant develops swollen hollow stems in which the ants live and inside which they farm scale insects, leaving the leaves undamaged.

Raising Caterpillars

It is our experience that many of the butterflies featured in this book are easy to hand-raise. Observing the emergence of a new caterpillar from an egg, the growth of a caterpillar through its four or five larval stages, its transformation into the chrysalis stage and the emergence of a butterfly, is very interesting. If you want to watch their whole process of development, you will need to protect the caterpillars from predators and parasites. A good way to do this is to bring them inside and hand-raise the caterpillars from eggs.

If you want to hand-raise caterpillars, it is important to note the caterpillars' behaviour when they are due to moult. Most caterpillars can be easily shifted to new leaves or new plants by using a soft artists' paintbrush. However, it is easy to accidentally interrupt their moult cycle and perhaps kill the caterpillars if they are shifted at certain critical stages. Different species take very different amounts of time for moulting. If you observe a caterpillar sitting still without eating for some time, hours, even days, leave it alone and don't shift it.

Caterpillars can be raised in a number of ways, which are best determined by how their host plant reacts to being picked. Some types of caterpillar food (leaves, flowers, or other parts) may wilt quickly and deteriorate, making them unsuitable for picking. In such cases potted plants need to be used. Some people simply choose to leave the caterpillars outside, on their host plants, and cover the part of the plant with a netting sleeve. Two methods for raising caterpillars indoors will be described here.

With food sources that last well after being picked, caterpillars of many species can be raised reasonably easily in small containers such as well-washed take-away food containers. Caterpillars do not have the same requirements for breathing that warm-blooded animals do, so a small container that is opened on a number of occasions each day is not a problem. Keeping the lid closed stops the leaves from drying out and also any ants from getting in. Unless you are raising a gregarious species, use these containers for small numbers of caterpillars only. With some species, regular contact with others of their own or another kind, or a shortage of food, can result in cannibalism.

Regularly replace the food in the container to keep it as fresh as possible, Also, clean out the caterpillar frass (the eliminated digested leaves, now compost). Opening the lid for cleaning and replacing food refreshes the air, and reduces any build-up of mould.

In the case where you run out of food for your caterpillars, at times you can substitute another known host plant. However, this can also arrest the caterpillars' development, some-times leading to its death. Knowing when substitution is possible comes with experience.

Spray the inside of the lid of the container with a little water to help maintain the freshness of the food. This is also useful because, occasionally, caterpillars also need to drink a little water. Lining the bottom of the container with tissue to absorb any extra moisture can also help keep the caterpillars healthy.

Where the food supply deteriorates quickly, it is more appropriate to raise the caterpillars on small potted plants of the required species. These may need to be rotated with other plants of the same species from outside because some plants do not tolerate low light situations. Plastic aquariums stood up on their sides with netting for the cover work well enough in the short term. Some people obtain polystyrene boxes with lids for the purpose. They stand the box on its short side and cut much of the lid away, replacing the opening with fly screen. Alternatively people can buy or construct netting structures that are placed over the plant brought indoors. Purpose-built kits complete with plants and caterpillars are available for classroom use. This live food method can be used for hand-rearing all of the butterflies. It is the only successful method for the Tailed Emperor.

As can be seen from the photos in the coloured section, caterpillars form chrysalises in four main ways. The larger butterflies either suspend themselves by their rear end and hang upside down (some Browns, Nymphs and Danaids) or they suspend themselves by their rear end and support themselves with a silk girdle about one third of the way down their body from their head (Swallowtails, Whites and Yellows). Skippers, Flats, Awls, Darts and some other Browns frequently pupate or form their chrysalises in the leaf shelters that their caterpillars construct or loose in the leaf litter. The Blues, Coppers, Jewels, Azures and Hairstreaks are mostly small butterflies that pupate against leaves or bark, in ants nests or shelters, or in the ground. Knowing which of these groups your caterpillar belongs to can help you work out what to do when your caterpillars are getting ready to transform into chrysalises.

When the time arrives to transform into a chrysalis, several changes are noticeable. They stop eating and often either become restless, spending much time walking around the container, or they sit very still. At this time they show some colour change and become more translucent. No matter how or where the caterpillar transforms, once it emerges as a new butterfly, it needs sufficient room to expand its wings. This is particularly important for the larger butterflies that hang down to do this. These groups are the Swallowtails, Whites, Yellows, Browns, Nymphs and Danaines. The other groups of smaller butterflies are able to pump up their wings in smaller spaces.

With experience, I know some caterpillars might form their chrysalis on the side of a small container, particularly if they are Swallowtails, Whites or Yellows. Once theses types of caterpillars start showing the changes, I shift them to a larger container with upright or diagonally placed sticks in it, to give them a surface on which for form chrysalises. Then, if necessary, the chrysalis can be moved to make sure that the newly emerging butterfly will have sufficient space. If the chrysalis has formed on the lid of the container by its rear end, I remove the lid and place it over a deeper container.

Whichever method you choose, it is important to make sure that no stage of the lifecycle is exposed to direct heat or sunlight. This is particularly so if you are keeping them in small containers,as these quickly become solar cookers and the caterpillars aren't able to survive. If you have them inside make sure the house is well-ventilated on hot days.

Ecological Relationships and Population Cycles

The Monarch butterfly's lifecycle is well-known. Less well-known is how useful one of this butterfly's host plants, the Silkpod or Milkweed (*Asclepias curassavica*), can be in demonstrating some of the relationships between animals in the natural environment.

To examine these relationships it may be helpful to use a hand lens since this allows a better view of the smaller creatures. The extra magnification provided is quite interesting for children, in particular, who often apply the scrutiny of the lens to many other things.

In our garden, in most years, early spring brings a population explosion of a yellow species of aphid on the Silkpods. As the plants begin to show signs of being seriously affected due to the large numbers of these insects, careful observation of the plants will show a number of other insects taking a very active interest in the plants.

A small fly, with a stripey yellow and black abdomen, and a delightful way of being able to stand still in space, and apparently move backwards, forwards and sideways, starts frequenting the plants. These are known as Hover Flies. Some time later a careful examination of the aphids will show small slug-like larvae in their midst. These maggots are eating the aphids, and when mature, form pupae in the ground and emerge as new Hover Flies.

Often you can also observe Ladybeetles taking a great interest in the plants. Females lay their small, elongated yellow eggs in groups of around twenty or so. These hatch into ravenous aphid eaters, grow through several moults and eventually pupate on the plants. In about a week an adult Ladybeetle emerges to mate and continue the cycle.

The aphids also attract a small black species of wasp. These lay their eggs in the aphids themselves. After a while a number of larger, round, darker coloured aphids appear on the plant. Close examination may reveal a small hole in them. Adult wasps have emerged from these, now dead, aphids to also continue their lifecycle.

As these predatory species build up their numbers, the number of aphids declines. Eventually there are more predators to be seen than aphids. Once this happens the mature stages of the predators quickly disappear, presumably to try to find another feast somewhere else.

Another population cycle that can be observed with this plant involves the butterfly itself. If you have a group of plants they can grow happily (once the aphids decline) for a long time without attracting the butterflies. However, sooner or later, a mated female Monarch will find the plants. She will take up residence, floating from plant to plant, laying eggs for some days. Slowly but surely the caterpillars start to hatch, eat ravenously, moult on four or five occasions in about a week, metamorphose into a chrysalis for about a week, and then emerge as a butterfly. The females and males mate quickly, and the female starts the lifecycle once again. The numbers of caterpillars can quickly build up. Progressively they start completely defoliating the plants. As their numbers build, the attention of caterpillar-eating wasps and Tachinid Flies is attracted. Wasps carry off small caterpillars to their nests.

Tachinid flies appear (see p. 13) and lay their eggs on the caterpillars. Their eggs are very sticky and remain visible on the surface of the caterpillar until its next moult. The fly larvae eat the insides of the caterpillar and chrysalis and emerge as pupae of their own from the chrysalis. They leave a tell-tale small hole and a thin thread hanging from the chrysalis. As this parasite's population builds it becomes hard to find a caterpillar that hasn't had an egg laid on it. This is probably for the best as, by now, the caterpillars have done a really good job of plant control and there's little, if any, food left for the next generation.

Nectar Plants

There are stories told about butterflies emerging, mating, laying eggs and dying before eating or drinking. This does not apply to any of the 48 butterflies featured in this book, all of which need a source of sugar to fuel their flight. Our butterflies mostly get their fuel from nectar in flowers, though a few use oozing sap or juice from damaged or fallen fruit.

When it comes to nectar plants for butterflies, many people are influenced by experience from other countries and plant exotics. They grow things like Buddleias, Pentas, Verbenas, etc. These work quite well, though some care needs to be taken in picking the particular variety. Many of these plants have been bred and hybridized over many years. They have been selected for showy flowers and have been hand-pollinated, so they may have lost some nectar producing ability, and the ability to attract pollinators. This loss of ability to support wildlife in modern plants has been increasingly noticed in Europe. So, if you want to use exotic plants, you need to pick a variety that you have seen frequented by insects, or that is recommended by someone who has tried it.

Herb and vegetable gardens have many plants that provide nectar for butterflies as well as many local native bees. Even the humble onion has flowers that are used by the Common Crow.

There are many native plants that provide nectar for butterflies. Lime Berry (*Micromelum minutum*) is well known for attracting many butterflies and so is Sweet Bursaria (*Bursaria spinosa*). The difficult to grow Tall Rice Flower (*Pimelea ligustrina*) is also quite attractive, as is the easy to grow vine, Monkey Rope (*Parsonsia straminea*). Many gum trees also produce copious nectar, but this often passes unnoticed as the flowers are high up in the canopy. Rough Apple (*Angophora floribunda*) or Water Gum (*Tristaniopsis laurina*) are trees which, if planted near a balcony, are likely to produce a good show.

There are many great nectar plants out in the bush waiting to be discovered. Unfortunately, not many people get out there to see them. This can be partly remedied by reading books written by people with this knowledge. Keith Williams' "*Plants of Queeensland*" mentions over 60 plants that have flowers that are attractive to butterflies or other insects.

Another solution is to bring more native plants into urban areas where there are more eyes to observe them. David Barnes has had a wildlife garden at Brackenridge in Brisbane for over twenty years. He has planted a diverse range of plants for a variety of animals. During this time he has noticed that some plants like Spindly Baeckea (*Babingtonia crenulata*) attract many types of butterflies, Paper Daisies (*Xerochrysum bracteatum*) attract Australian Painted Lady and Common Crow butterflies. Little Evodia (*Melicope rubra*, formerly *Evodiella muelleri*) attracts Blue Triangle butterflies.

If you do happen to observe butterflies in their natural habitat, you will probably notice that they will utilize a nearby nectar plant. This will not always be the largest or showiest plant. If you do have a few favourite butterflies, find them in the wild and see what their favoured nectar plants are.

So, whether you have a manicured garden of exotics or a wildlife garden, you have a great variety of nectar plants to choose from.

Further reading: Barnes, D. J. and Moran, A. (2001). *Fauna Friendly Plants of South East Queensland*. Brisbane: The Authors. Phone: 3261 4034
    Williams, K. (1979 - 1999). *Plants of Queensland* (in 4 volumes). North Ipswich: The Author.

Day-flying Moths (mostly)

When the subject turns to butterflies the first question that most people ask is, "What does that huge caterpillar eating my (insert your plant here, eg. Impatiens) turn into?" If the caterpillar has a curved spike on its rear end it usually turns into one of the species of Hawk Moths. There are at least 59 species of these moths in Australia, including four species that have clear wings, look like large bees, fly during the day, and are known as Bee-hawk Moths. One of these Bee-hawk Moths has caterpillars that feed on Gardenias or related natives like *Pavetta australiensis*. When mature, the caterpillar descends to the ground and spins a flimsy cocoon amongst the dead leaves.

Another thing people ask about is the difference between a butterfly and a moth. There is no easy answer to this. Butterflies generally fly during the day and have clubbed rather than feathery antenna. Moth caterpillars often spin a silken cocoon around their pupae, whereas butterflies usually have naked pupae or chrysalises. Moths have a structure called a frenulum that couples their wings during flight. For a technical explanation see Common (1990) *"Moths of Australia"*, page 24, column 1, line 45 and the Figure 14.2 on page 22. There are exceptions to all these. For instance, there are dusk and night-flying butterflies and day-flying moths. There is a butterfly, the Regent Skipper, where the male's frenulum would make it a moth and the female's lack of frenulum would make it a butterfly.

One of the most spectacular day-flying moths is the Josephs Coat Moth (*Agarista agricola*), which is illustrated on the back cover. The caterpillars are quite impressive too, with their orange and white markings and unusual paddle-shaped hairs. Adult males sometimes make a clicking sound while flying. The caterpillars feed on Slender Grape (*Cayratia clematidea*) or Forest Grape (*Cissus opaca*). Both these vines produce large tubers and should not be planted near brickwork or paths. The Slender Grape also suckers freely and produces a new tuber under each sucker. Some Hawk Moth caterpillars and caterpillars of another day-flying moth, *Cruria donowani*, also feed on it.

Hawk Moth   HS
Theretra latreillei

Hawk Moth caterpillar on Native Mulberry HS
Gnathothlibus erotus

Privet Hawk Moth (white, black & grey) HS
Psilogramma menefron

Day-flying moth caterpillar,   HS
ready to pupate
Cruria donowani

Day-flying moth drinking water   HS
Cruria donowani

Bee-hawk Moth caterpillar   HS
Cephonodes hylas

Bee-hawk Moth adult   HS
Cephonodes hylas

Brisbane's most common day-flying moth is the Magpie Moth (*Nyctemera amicus*). Its hairy caterpillars feed on a common weed in suburban areas called Thickhead (*Crassocephalum crepidioides*). It also feeds on the native Rockledge Daisy (*Gynura drymophila*) (see p. 14).

The delightful Satin-green Forester (*Pollanisus viridipulverulenta*) is a small day-flying moth with metallic blue-green wings. Its caterpillars feed at night on Guinea Flowers (*Hibbertia* spp.) and have been found at Karawatha Forest by Thomas Creevey.

There are many others, for example: a small speckled moth (*Utetheisa pulchelloides*) whose caterpillars feed on Blue Heliotrope (*Heliotropium amplexicaule*); Mistletoe Moth (*Comocrus behri*) a large black, white and red moth whose caterpillars feed on mistletoes; a small orange moth (*Argina astrea*) whose caterpillars feed on Rattlepods (*Crotalaria* spp.).

Though not day-flying, a moth that sometimes causes concern is the Granny's Cloak Moth (*Speiredonia spectans*). It is a large brown moth with a purple sheen and very conspicuous eyespots. It often enters houses where it hides in dark corners and cupboards. Despite its name and its behaviour, neither it, nor its caterpillars, eat clothes. A caterpillar of this moth was found by John Moss. It was feeding on Yellow Tulip (*Drypetes deplanchei*) at Townsville. The caterpillar was similar to the caterpillar of the Old Lady or Granny Moth (*Dasypodia selenophora*) found in Southern Australia.

According to Ian Common (1990), there were about 10,000 named species of moths of an estimated 22,000 species in total. This main text on moths is about 540 pages in one volume, and covers a limited number of moths per family. Compare this with the approximately 400 species of butterflies in Australia. The main text, "*Butterflies of Australia*", by Michael Braby (2000) occupies two volumes comprising 976 pages, and covers every known butterfly. So don't be alarmed if that "butterfly" does not appear in any of the butterfly books - it may be a moth.

Resources

Barnes, D. J. and Moran, A. (2001). *Fauna Friendly Plants of South East Queensland*. Brisbane: The Authors.

Braby, Michael F. (2000). *Butterflies of Australia: their identification, biology and distribution.* (in 2 volumes). Collingwood, Vic.: CSIRO Publishing.

Braby, Michael F. (2004). *The Complete Field Guide to Butterflies of Australia.* Canberra: CSIRO Publishing.

Butterfly & Other Invertebrates Club (1997). *Swallowtails of south east Queensland and northern New South Wales* [a poster]. Runcorn, Qld: The Club.

Chew, Peter. *Brisbane Insects and Spiders* [website]. I: http://brisbaneinsects.com/pchew_brisbane/index.htm

Common, I. F. B. (1990). *Moths of Australia*. Carlton, Vic.: Melbourne University Press.

Conondale Range Committee (2004). *Walking on the Wilder Side ... in the Conondales.* The Committee.

Cubberla Witton Catchments Network. I: http://cwcn.org.au/index.php/biodiversity

Grund, R. *South Australian Butterflies & Moths* [website]. I: https://sabutterflies.org.au/home/index.html

Herbison-Evans, Don and Crossley, Stella. *The Identification of Caterpillars of Australia* [website]. I: http://lepidoptera.butterflyhouse.com.au/faqs/ident.html

Horton, H. ed. (2002). *A Brisbane Bushland: the history and natural history of Enoggera Reservoir and its environs.* Brisbane, Queensland Naturalists' Club Inc.

McDonald, G. (2004). *Grow Natives on the Gold Coast: a practical guide for gardeners.* Nerang : Society for Growing Australian Plants (Qld Region) Inc. Gold Coast Branch.

Moss, John T. (2019). *Butterfly Host Plants of south-east Queensland and northern New South Wales.* 4th ed. Brisbane: Butterfly & Other Invertebrates Club Inc.

Museum Victoria. Collections [Victorian Butterflies] [website] I: https://collections.museumvictoria.com.au/search?query=Victorian+Butterflies&recordtype=species

Palmwoods Arts and Crafts Group (2001). *Wings over the Sunshine Coast: Naturalists and Artists describe our Birds and Butterflies.* The Group.

Sankowsky, Gary ([2002]). *A Garden on the Wing: Attracting birds and butterflies to your garden.* Tolga, Qld: Zodiac Publications. I: www.rainforestmagic.com.au

Williams, K. (1979 -1999). *Plants of Queensland* (in 4 volumes). North Ipswich: The Author.

Index

Contacts

Australian Museum,
6 College St., Sydney, NSW 2010
I: australianmuseum.net.au/;
Phone: 02 9320 6202 for Search and
Discover or 02 9320 6000 for general
enquiries.

Brisbane City Council, Mt Coot-tha
Library, Mt Coot-tha Rd., Toowong,
QLD 4066; Phone: 3403 8888

Butterfly & Other Invertebrates Club Inc.,
PO Box 2113, Runcorn, QLD 4113;
I: www.boic.org.au

Entomological Society of Queensland
PO Box 537, Indooroopilly, QLD
4068
I: www.esq.org.au/

Native Plants Queensland (formerly
Society for Growing Australian Plants),
PO Box 586, Fortitude Valley, QLD 4006;
I: npq.org.au/

Queensland Museum Inquiry Centre,
cnr. Grey & Melbourne Sts., South
Bank, QLD, 4101; phone: 3840 7555;
I: www.qm.qld.gov.au/

Queensland Naturalist's Club Inc.,
PO Box 5663, West End, QLD 4101;
I: qnc.org.au/

Wildlife Preservation Society of Qld,
95 William St., Brisbane, QLD 4000;
I: wildlife.org.au/

Interstate groups

WA: Western Australian Insect Study
Society Inc. c/- Western Australian
Museum, Francis St., Perth, WA 6000
I: museum.wa.gov.au/waiss/

SA: Butterfly Conservation SA Inc.
c/- South Australian Museum, North
Tce., Adelaide, SA 5000;
I: butterflyconservationsa.net.au/

NSW: The Society for Insect Studies, 12
Park Ave., Roseville, NSW, 2069.
I: http://www.duttcom.com/Insects/
index.php

Tas: Tasmanian Field Naturalists Club
Inc. PO Box 68A, Hobart, Tasmania,
7250
I: https://www.tasfieldnats.org.au/

Vic: Entomological Society of Victoria,
56 Looker Rd., Montmorency, Vic.
3094
I: entsocvic.org.au/

The Field Naturalists Club of Victoria Inc.
Locked Bag 3, Blackburn, Vic. 3130.
I: www.fncv.org.au/

Butterfly businesses

Butterfly Encounters – Ross Kendall,
butterfly releases for special occasions
and educational kits and resources.
I: www.butterflyencounters.com.au/

Coff's Harbour Butterfly House -
butterfly display, maze, tea rooms, gift
shop and woodturning display
I: www.butterflyhouse.com.au

Earthling Enterprises PL - speaking,
books, consultancy, lifecycle signs
PO Box 5167, West End, Qld 4101
I: www.earthling.com.au

Lois Hughes, Artist. 163 West Mt. Cotton
Rd., Mt Cotton, QLD 4163, phone:
3206 6229 for original commissions,
cards and prints.

Mt Glorious Biological Centre - Katie &
Tony Hiller, Insect livestock and
specimens, insect workshops at
schools.
I: www.mountgloriousbutterflies.com

Other sources

Facebook pages:
Australian butterflies and moths:
https://www.facebook.com/groups/
799465170167144/2817545805025727

Butterfly & Other Invertebrates Club:
https://www.facebook.com/groups/
187619097411/

and so many more - Yay! finally taking off